Knowledge Based

Management

Unleashing the Power
of Quality Improvement

ABOUT THE AUTHORS

Stephen R. Schmidt served for 20 years in the U.S. Air Force: 10 years as an instructor pilot and 10 years as a tenured professor at the USAF Academy. Dr. Schmidt has more than 20 years of teaching and consulting experience at the Academy, several other universities, and industries around the world. His "Keep It Simple Statistically" (KISS) approach has gained him widespread popularity and an impressive list of clients: General Electric, Sony, Motorola, Boeing, Texas Instruments, Lockheed Martin, AlliedSignal, Levi Strauss, Advanced Microdevices, Abbott Labs, Citicorp, Ford, Dannon, Delco Electronics (Delnosa-Mexico), National Semiconductor, plus many others. Because of his vast experience, he has served as an adjunct faculty member to the *Motorola Six Sigma Research Institute* where he trained the first wave of Black Belts at Motorola and Texas Instruments. In addition, he served on the Board of Directors for the Statistical Applications Institute and he is currently a senior partner for Air Academy Associates. He is also an adjunct professor at The University of Texas at Austin. He earned a B.S. in Math at the USAF Academy, an M.S. in Operations Research at the University of Texas, and a Ph.D. in Applied Statistics at the University of Northern Colorado. Dr. Schmidt also co-authored three recent texts: *Understanding Industrial Designed Experiments; Basic Statistics: Tools for Continuous Improvement;* and *Total Quality: A Textbook of Strategic Quality, Leadership and Planning.*

Mark J. Kiemele served for 20 years in the U.S. Air Force: 8 years as a scientific analyst in research and development and 12 years as a tenured professor at the USAF Academy. Dr. Kiemele has more than 25 years of teaching experience and has educated and trained more than 8,000 scientists, engineers, managers, trainers, practitioners, and college students. He has supported the design and development of many highly technical systems, including the Maverick and Cruise Missile systems. He specializes in teaching statistical methods to nonstatisticians. His clients include Microsoft, Sony, General Electric, AlliedSignal, Lockheed Martin, EG&G, Coilcraft, Corning, Data General, Chevron, Walker Parking, and Abbott Laboratories. Dr. Kiemele is a senior partner with Air Academy Associates. He earned a B.S. and M.S. in Mathematics from North Dakota State University and a Ph.D. in Computer Science from Texas A & M University. Dr. Kiemele has co-authored the book *Basic Statistics: Tools for Continuous Improvement* and the AT&T Bell Labs book entitled *Network Modeling, Simulation, and Analysis.* He also edited the book *Understanding Industrial Designed Experiments.*

Ronald J. Berdine served more than 20 years in the U.S. Air Force where he served as an Electronic Warfare Officer, Navigator, Associate Professor and most recently as Head of the Department of Mathematical Sciences at the USAF Academy. He teaches and consults on the subject of applications of statistical methods. He is an experienced facilitator in the areas of problem solving, metric development, and implementation of process improvement strategies. His clients include Bombardier, Sony, General Electric, AlliedSignal, Atmel, Motorola, Abbott Labs, Lenox, AB Dick and numerous Department of Defense Agencies. He is co-author of the text *Basic Statistics: Tools for Continuous Improvement.* He received his B.S. in Mathematics from Iowa State University, his M.S. in Operations Research from Stanford University, and his Ph.D. in Statistics from Texas A&M University. He is now a senior partner with Air Academy Associates.

OTHER TEXTS BY AIR ACADEMY PRESS & ASSOCIATES

Understanding Industrial Designed Experiments
4th Edition (1994)
by Stephen R. Schmidt and Robert G. Launsby. ISBN 1-880156-03-2

This is an applications oriented text which blends the competing Taguchi, Shainin, and classical approaches to designed experiments into a new and powerful approach for gaining knowledge. Rules of Thumb are emphasized to enable the reader to implement the techniques without being encumbered with mathematical complexity. Topics include: *Full and Fractional Factorials, Plackett-Burman, Box-Behnken, Central Composite, D-optimal, Mixture, Nested and Robust Designs.* Included are over 300 pages of actual industrial case studies from a wide variety of industries. Simulation software and the student version of the DOE KISS software package are also included.

Basic Statistics: Tools for Continuous Improvement
4th Edition (1997)
by M.J. Kiemele, S.R. Schmidt, and R.J. Berdine. ISBN 1-880156-06-7

This text provides a refreshingly new approach to applying statistical tools for moving up the quality improvement ladder. Emphasis is on "statistical thinking" for transforming data into information, plus applications. Topics include: *Statistics and the Total Quality Movement; Steps Before Collecting Data; Descriptive Statistics; Probability Distributions; Confidence Intervals; Hypothesis Testing; Analysis of Variance; Regression; Design of Experiments; Statistical Process Control; Gage Capability; Multivariate Charts; Reliability; and Quality Function Deployment.* More than 65 examples and case studies, contributed by more than 10 industrial practitioners, span manufacturing, service, software, government, and the health care industries. Included is the student version of SPC KISS, a very user friendly statistical applications software package.

Beyond Survival: Creating Prosperity Through People
(1995)
by Robert B. Blaha. ISBN 1-880156-04-0

This guide to High Performance Work Systems (HPWS) details the steps involved in forming work groups, assessing needs, setting goals, implementing strategies, and measuring results. Written for those who want to maximize employee potential, the text uses histories and informative examples to describe the extraordinary impact of HPWS on earnings and customer satisfaction.

Knowledge Based Management

Unleashing the Power
of Quality Improvement

Stephen R. Schmidt
Mark J. Kiemele
Ronald J. Berdine

Air Academy Press & Associates
Colorado Springs, CO

Library of Congress Catalog Card Number: 95-83869

ISBN 1-880156-05-9

Printed in the United States of America
9 8 7 6 5 4   – 01 00 99 98

The authors recognize that perfection is unattainable without continuous improvement. Therefore, we solicit comments as to how to improve this text. To relay your comments or to obtain further information, contact:

AIR ACADEMY PRESS & ASSOCIATES,LLC
1155 Kelly Johnson Blvd., Suite 105
Colorado Springs, CO 80920
Phone: (719) 531-0777
FAX: (719) 531-0778
e-mail: aapa@airacad.com
website: www.airacad.com

To our wives and families who have made many sacrifices as we continue our quest to help industry obtain a return on investment from continuous quality improvement.

Table of Contents

PREFACE   xi

ACKNOWLEDGEMENTS   xiii

CHAPTER 1
    INTRODUCTION TO KNOWLEDGE BASED
    MANAGEMENT   1

CHAPTER 2
    MOTIVATING THE NEED FOR QUALITY
    IMPROVEMENT AND KNOWLEDGE   9

CHAPTER 3
    PHILOSOPHIES FOR GETTING STARTED   21
        Deming   24
        Juran   28
        Ishikawa   30
        Knowledge Based Management   31

CHAPTER 4
    IMPLEMENTATION STRATEGIES   67
        PDCA   80
        FOCUS   82
        Questions Managers Need to Ask   88

CHAPTER 5
    BASIC TOOLS AND TECHNIQUES TO OBTAIN
    KNOWLEDGE   123
        Affinity Diagram   124
        Benchmarking   126
        Cause and Effect Diagram   127
        Common Sense   130
        Failure Mode and Effects Analysis (FMEA)   132
        Fault Tree Analysis   134
        Histogram   135
        Input-Process-Output (IPO) Diagram   137
        Measures of Central Tendency   139
        Measures of Dispersion   141

Nominal Group Technique 142
Pareto Chart 144
Process Capability Measurements 146
Process Flow Diagram 149
Quality Function Deployment (QFD) 152
Run Chart 153
Scatter Diagram 154
Teamwork 157

CHAPTER 6
ADVANCED TOOLS AND TECHNIQUES TO OBTAIN
KNOWLEDGE 163
Statistical Process Control (SPC) 166
Design of Experiments (DOE) 177

CHAPTER 7
KBM: A MODERN QUALITY IMPROVEMENT PARADIGM
ISO-9000, QS-9000, D1-9000, Process
Validation, Process Characterization,
Quality Systems Review, Baldrige Criteria
vs KBM 187

APPENDIX A
Questions Managers Need to Answer A - 1

APPENDIX B
Questions Managers Need to Ask B - 1

APPENDIX C
Change Management C - 1

APPENDIX D
Six Sigma for Manufacturing and Non-Manufacturing
Processes D - 1

GLOSSARY G - 1

REFERENCES R - 1

INDEX I - 1

Preface

We believe that any manager at any level who wants to improve his or her organization's bottom line will benefit from reading this text. It gives a manager a real hands-on approach to quality improvement. In this text, *quality improvement* means to deliver *better, faster, and lower cost products and services*. Managers are often frustrated and sometimes intimidated by the complexity of modern-day processes and feel helpless to do anything about it. This book provides managers with an action plan they can implement immediately.

The text presents a philosophy and strategy for unleashing the power of quality improvement. It is not our purpose to present an alternative approach to Deming, Juran, or Ishikawa. Instead, we build upon a common, underlying theme that is clearly present in their work. That theme is **knowledge**. Deming even used the phrase "profound knowledge" in his teaching and writing. While the philosophies of these and other quality gurus typically have emphasized the "whats" of quality improvement, this text focuses on the "hows." Knowledge about processes, products, and people is shown to be the atomic makeup of quality improvement. How we get the right kinds of knowledge is the heart of the text. Getting the right kinds of knowledge requires asking the right kinds of questions. We provide managers with two sets of questions they can use to focus on the proper knowledge base: "*Questions Managers Need to Answer*" and "*Questions Managers Need to Ask.*" Of course, questions without the correct answers yield little knowledge. Thus, we have provided the tools and techniques needed to properly answer the questions.

This book is not only about learning how to gain knowledge about our processes, products, and people, it's also about **why** we need to do so. It's about quality improvement, return on investment, improving the bottom line, long-term success, and increased job security. It's about why some organizations succeed in their quality improvement efforts and others do not. It's about giving managers something concrete they can use **now** to drive the quality culture. In this light, we show that knowledge is a key ingredient to the Six Sigma initiatives at General Electric, Sony, and other companies that have successfully embraced the Six Sigma business strategy. We present a Six Sigma Project Master Strategy that establishes a methodology in which these knowledge producing questions can repeatedly make a positive impact on a company's bottom line.

Writing this text was only slightly more difficult than choosing a title. We wanted to use phrases such as "A Common Sense Approach," "Asking the Right Questions," and "Solving the Quality Improvement Puzzle," all of which describe the contents. However, our experience has indicated that the major barrier for success in most organizations is the lack of knowledge about processes, products, and people. Without an adequate knowledge base, it is difficult to communicate and to make good decisions. Without knowledge, we develop a culture of diversity—diverse opinions! We know that if we can help managers close this knowledge gap, we will have provided a valuable service. Thus, the name "Knowledge Based Management."

The last thing we want to do is complicate the life of a manager. Therefore, we have made every effort to provide you with something extremely simple, yet radically different, with enough common sense and practicality that you can apply immediately to make quality improvement a reality in your organization. After you have read and digested this text, all you need is the will to win. As the Starship Enterprise Captain Jean-Luc Picard would say: "*Make It So.*"

Stephen R. Schmidt   *Mark J. Kiemele*   *Ronald J. Berdine*

Colorado Springs, CO

July 1998

Acknowledgements

Winston Churchill once said, "Writing a book is an adventure. To begin with, it is a toy and an amusement. Then it becomes a mistress, then it becomes a master, then it becomes a tyrant. The last phase is that just as you are about to be reconciled to your servitude, you kill the monster and fling him about to the public."

We wish to thank our families, friends, and colleagues mentioned below for their part in helping us "slay the monster." Without them, we would have been "devoured." Each provided valuable comments and constructive criticism that aided us immensely, and their encouragement provided us the inspiration to complete the battle.

Mr. Thayer Allison (*Compassion International*)
Dr. Diane Arnold (*ARAMARK Educational Resources*)
Dr. Bill Brown (*Abbott Laboratories*)
Ms. Jeanne Brown (*SCI Systems, Inc.*)
Dr. Kenneth Case (*Oklahoma State University*)
Mr. Tony Chrest (*Walker Parking Consultants/Engineers, Inc.*)
Mr. Mark S. Davis (*Honeywell*)
Mr. Steve Dempsey (*Interactive Process Technology*)
Mr. Mike Lovitt (*Tessco Group, Inc.*)
Mr. Loren Root (*Motorola*)
Ms. Lisa Reagan (*AlliedSignal*)
Mr. Ed Robertson (*Human Capital Associates*)
Ms. Bonnie Workman (*A.B. Dick Company*)

We wish to express a special thanks to our associates, Susan Darby, Jon Dukeman, Suellen Hill, Carol Kiemele, and Beatriz Orozco, for their honesty, patience, and diligence in getting this book published. Even their unsolicited suggestions contributed mightily.

Special recognition is due Mr. Ken Mooney *(K.M. Consulting, Inc.)* and Dr. Tom Cheek (*Raytheon TI Systems*), who went well beyond the call of duty. Ken contributed countless hours of writing, editing, and critiquing the manuscript, offering entirely new sections where gaping holes existed. Tom contributed Appendix C, a very timely and original treatment on change management. Their work is tremendously appreciated.

Thank you to Bernard Sandoval of the Muir Agency in Colorado Springs for the cover design which so vividly evokes the imagery of the power of quality improvement.

Finally, we wish to thank God for giving us such patient and understanding families. Their support, as always, was unwavering throughout this endeavor.

Chapter 1

INTRODUCTION TO KNOWLEDGE BASED MANAGEMENT

"Wise men store up knowledge..."

Prov 10:14

For the past several years industry has been bombarded with a plethora of quality improvement philosophies, tools, and techniques which are often not fully explained or synthesized in a way that clearly depicts the *"Big Picture."* It seems like there has been a constant push to generate more and more pieces for the quality improvement puzzle without sufficient information on how to put them all together properly. See Figure 1.1. Furthermore, the motivation to effectively pursue quality

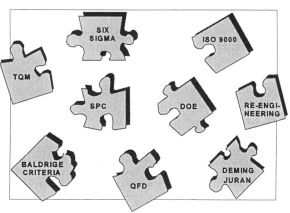

Figure 1.1 The Quality Improvement Puzzle:
"A Set of Disjointed Pieces?" or "Do the Pieces Fit Together?"

improvement has been impaired by not fully understanding that quality improvement means **Better, Faster and Lower Cost Products and Services** and by the decade-long American corporate strategy of massive consolidation and downsizing at unprecedented rates. It appears that no job is secure. Is it any wonder that many people, managers in particular, have become disillusioned about the value of pursuing any further efforts in quality improvement?

The *Wall Street Journal* (October 1, 1992) article "Total Quality is only Partial Success" documents many of the Total Quality Management (TQM) frustrations that are prevalent today. A barometer for today's interest in TQM is the number of applicants for the Malcolm Baldrige National Quality Award. According to the National Institute of Standards, the number of applicants is falling off. Figure 1.2 shows a definite decline in the last six years. In addition, there were no winners from service companies in 1995 nor from small businesses in 1995 and 1997. Not since 1989 has there been an absence of winners in these categories.

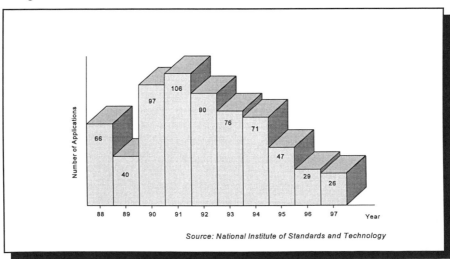

Figure 1.2 Applications for the Malcolm Baldrige Award

According to a statement from David Garvin (Harvard Business School and former Baldrige examiner) in the *USA Today* (October 17, 1995) article "Is TQM Dead?", "There's a set of companies like Intel, Motorola, L.L. Bean, and AT&T where quality is part of the fabric. There's another set of companies where quality was the fad of the month. They have moved on to other things."

What makes one company's quality improvement efforts successful and another one's unsuccessful? We will address this question throughout the text and provide a common sense approach that leads to success. Basically, a business unit needs the ability to answer questions like:

> *Where are we?*
>
> *Where are we going?*
>
> *How will we get there?*

Acquiring the knowledge to answer these questions can help motivate the action that will produce return on investment from quality improvement efforts.

Webster's dictionary defines **knowledge** as: **familiarity, awareness, or understanding gained through experience or study.** In order to evaluate our knowledge base, we have developed two sets of detailed questions. First, to evaluate our knowledge of the management philosophies that lead to industrial competitiveness and success, we will present a list of **Questions Managers Need to Answer.** Then, to evaluate our knowledge of how to provide products and services **better**, **faster**, and at **lower cost**, we will present a list of **Questions Managers Need to Ask.** These questions, plus the tools and techniques needed to answer these critical questions, are the key ingredients for **Knowledge Based Management.** See Figure 1.3.

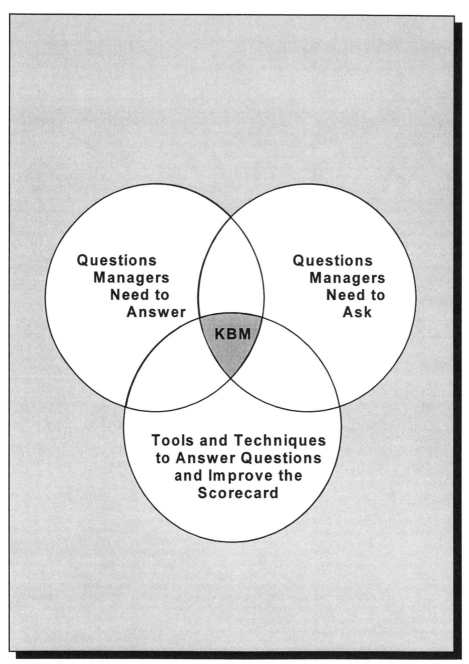

Figure 1.3 Key Ingredients for Knowledge Based Management (KBM)

Good decisions, based more on knowledge than opinion, must be supported with facts and data. Obtaining knowledge from facts and data will require the use of statistics; however, statistics is often taught as an "end" rather than a simple "means" to the real end which is **knowledge**. Many non-statistically oriented practitioners want to be able to gain knowledge without being bothered by statistical complexity. There are also those who dislike or distrust statistics because of how it has traditionally been taught or because they believe the well-circulated notion that "there are lies, damned lies, and statistics." It is our goal to revolutionize the communication of statistics. Our "Keep It Simple Statistically" (KISS) approach has gained international appeal because it produces large gains in knowledge from low levels of statistical complexity. See Figure 1.4.

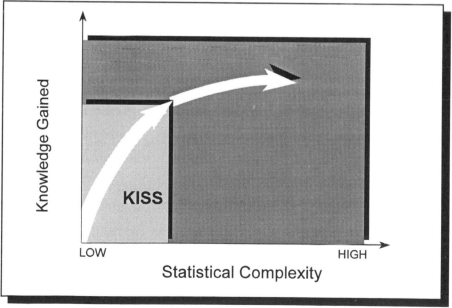

Figure 1.4 Why Advocate a KISS Approach?

Statisticians who insist on complicating every application often confuse their customers (managers, scientists, engineers, technicians, etc.) and usually end up in one of the following situations: i) out of a job, ii) constantly battling with their customers, or iii) isolated as an analyst who simply sits in a corner crunching data.

An apparent advocate of our KISS philosophy is Mr. Craig Barrett, President and COO at Intel. In his keynote address to a 1989 Accreditation Board for Engineering and Technology (ABET) conference, Mr. Barrett made the following statements:

- *"Statistical literacy is the key to our industrial competitiveness."*

- *"Instructors of statistics courses don't teach Applied Statistics."*

- *"Instructors of engineering courses don't teach statistics."*

- *"Engineering professors are not statistically literate."*

- *"The customer (industry) is NOT HAPPY."*

Craig Barrett

The conference was attended by many well-known Deans of Engineering, engineers, and statisticians. We at Air Academy Press & Associates (AAPA) were also represented at that conference and have responded to Mr. Barrett's challenging remarks with two KISS-oriented textbooks:

Basic Statistics: Tools for Continuous Improvement and *Understanding Industrial Designed Experiments*. To many, these texts take a radically new and refreshing approach to presenting statistical techniques, as the following quotes indicate:

"This is perhaps one of the most applicable and timely resources for engineers and managers..."

"The designs and methods are presented in a way that facilitates understanding and encourages the use of statistical techniques..."

"The format is ideal for managers and engineers."

"The text is easy to read, emphasizes applications, and contains material not usually found in introductory stats books..."

"The book has done a remarkably good job at reaching its intended audience of college level students taking their first course in statistics, as well as experienced managers and engineers..."

"Kudos to the authors for customer focus, something few authors ever consider beyond their own environment..."

Lest the reader be swayed that all comments have been positive, here are some "negative" comments:

"This is a strange book ... Statisticians will not find this book useful..."

"The absence of theory is a glaring weakness. The beauty of statistics is in its derivations and foundations, not in its use to 'get results'... there is too much emphasis on 'getting results'..."

Although these "negative" comments have been made about our philosophy and simplistic approach, the positives far outweigh the negatives, and the number of universities, companies, and organizations adopting our materials and/or services is growing rapidly. Our Six Sigma customers such as GE, Sony, AlliedSignal, Lockheed Martin, TI, and Corning, have adopted the KISS approach with a heavy emphasis on knowledge.

To extend this approach to management, we have developed a behavioral linkage between the tools and management. The new ideas we present are not academic in nature but stem from the successes we have had from training and consulting more than 50,000 practitioners around the world. It is our intent that the text be used as a common sense guide for managers, engineers, scientists, technicians, and analysts as they lead their organizations to "World Class" status.

Chapter 2

MOTIVATING THE NEED FOR QUALITY IMPROVEMENT AND KNOWLEDGE

"Knowledge has become the key economic resource and the dominant, if not the only, source of comparative advantage."

Peter Drucker

Quality improvement is not a fad forced upon us by our customers or a necessary evil imposed by some regulatory agency. Greater return on investment is being demanded by customers and society in general. The day is coming when even research scientists and educators will be held accountable for their activities. *Science* (Vol 269, July 1, 1995) reports that "a combination of arrogance and ignorance" is preventing the scientific research community from understanding who their customers are and why anyone would question the value of science's contribution to society. The Consortium on Productivity in the Schools (*USA Today*, August 30, 1995) reports that "American schools are not getting enough return on the $1.5 billion spent per school day on kindergarten through 12th grade education and need to find ways to increase efficiency and productivity." If we are to move forward, there needs to be sufficient emphasis on improved product and service quality. Quality improvement should be a critical part of any business strategy that is designed to generate maximum return on investment.

Over the last several years, many industries and specific companies have had severe problems. Table 2.1 reflects the consequences of these problems. Keep in mind that most of these companies had a quality improvement strategy in place at least 4 to 5 years prior to these layoffs. Obviously something was missing.

UGLY FACTS
OF THE 90'S

BOEING says it expects to cut about 8,000 jobs this year. (*USA Today*, 2/20/92)

IBM gave notice to thousands of employees who must find a job elsewhere in the company or leave with severance pay. IBM announced in December it will cut up to 20,000 jobs worldwide this year. (*USA Today*, 4/13/92)

GENERAL DYNAMICS confirmed that it will lay off 5,800 workers by the end of 1994. It has cut 10,000 workers since 1990. (*USA Today*, 7/30/92)

HEWLETT-PACKARD says it will trim about 2,700 jobs early next year through voluntary severance. (*USA Today*, 10/9/92)

DIGITAL EQUIPMENT CORP. plans to trim its workforce by 25,000 in the next few years. DEC cut 5,300 jobs last quarter. (*USA Today*, 10/15/92)

(Continued on next page)

Table 2.1 Ugly Facts of the 90's

GM BUYOUTS? **GM** plans to cut 54,000 hourly workers. It is under pressure to speed plans to close 21 plants and cut 74,000 jobs. (*USA Today*, 10/16/92)

THE FEDERAL DEPOSIT INSURANCE CORP. expects just over 100 banks to fail this year. About 85 banks have already failed this year. The FDIC expects 100 to 125 banks to fail next year. (*USA Today*, 10/19/92)

PRATT & WHITNEY will lay off 7,500 workers by the middle of next year, 4,800 more layoffs than previously announced. (*USA Today*, 10/19/92)

EASTMAN KODAK plans to lay off up to 3,000 workers. More than 8,000 workers left Kodak the past 18 months. (*USA Today*, 01/8/93)

MERCK earnings fell sharply in second quarter... cost cutting moves eliminate 2,100 jobs. (*Wall Street Journal*, 07/21/93)

JOHNSON & JOHNSON said it expects to eliminate 3,000 jobs. (*Wall Street Journal*, 08/12/93)

BRISTOL-MYERS SQUIBB projects 2,100 job cuts by 1994. (*Science*, 09/10/93)

WARNER-LAMBERT expects to cut 2,700 positions by 1996. (*Science*, 09/10/93)

RAYTHEON will pare 4,400 jobs or 7% of its workforce in the next two years. (*USA Today*, 10/03/94)

FLEET FINANCIAL plans to slash 5,000 jobs. (*USA Today*, 10/03/94)

AT&T announced it will lay off around 30,000 employees—mostly this year. (AP, *Gazette Telegraph*, Colorado Springs, CO, 1/5/96)

Table 2.1 Ugly Facts of the 90's

Many other layoffs and downsizings have taken place. However, U.S. industry is known for its ability to rebound. Several companies which have aggressively pursued a knowledge based quality improvement strategy have seen it positively affect the bottom line. Consider a *Business Week* study on the Malcolm Baldrige National Quality Award (MBNQA) which revealed that companies focused on quality (i.e., MBNQA winners) are realizing substantial growth in their stock value. Table 2.2 depicts the change in stock value from the time of the award to September 30, 1993, assuming $1,000 was invested at the time of award.

BALDRIGE PERFORMANCE		
COMPANY (Award Date)	Value on 9/30/93	Change*
AT&T (1992)	$ 1,217	21.7 %
AT&T (1992)	1,217	21.7 %
Federal Express (1990)	1,875	87.5 %
General Motors (1990)	1,219	21.9 %
IBM (1990)	372	-62.8 %
Motorola (1988)	5,423	442.3 %
Solectron (1991)	4,212	321.2 %
Texas Instruments (1992)	1,598	59.8 %
Westinghouse (1988)	525	-47.5 %
Xerox (1989)	1,263	26.3 %
Total	18,921	89.2 %
S&P 500	13,310	33.1 %

Table 2.2 Stock Value Changes for MBNQA Winners

(Source: Business Week)

---

*Note: The change represents a company-wide change while, in some cases, the Baldrige winner was a specific division within that company. The dual entry for AT&T indicates that two different divisions of AT&T won the award (in the same year).

The study points out that an equal investment in each of these MBNQA winners at the time of their announcement would have produced a cumulative return of 89.2% by September 30, 1993. Comparatively, an identical investment in the Standard and Poors 500 stocks over the same period would have produced only a 33.1% gain. Obviously, the Baldrige winners as a whole have shown remarkable success. We have seen similar results over a two-year period from some of our clients who have made a concerted effort to improve quality. See Table 2.3.

Clients of Air Academy Press & Associates	June 93 Stock Value Per Share	June 95 Stock Value Per Share
Texas Instruments	$ 70	$ 144
Motorola	43	65*
National Semiconductor	17	27
Atmel	13	53
McDonnell Douglas	21	76
Abbott Laboratories	25	41
Ford	26	30
Chevron	40	48
*Motorola had two 2-for-1 stock splits in this time period		

Table 2.3 Stock Value Gains for some of AAPA's Clients

In a 1994 *Total Quality Review* article by Defeo and Vecchio of the Juran Institute, Motorola's current and former top executives, George Fisher, Chris Galvin, and Gary Tooker, indicate that Motorola's Six Sigma quality efforts have resulted in the following:

> - *reduced in-process defect levels by a factor of 200 during the seven-year period 1987-1994;*
>
> - *saved a significant amount of the cost of manufacturing—$1.4 billion;*
>
> - *increased employee production on a dollar sales basis by 126 percent; and*
>
> - *increased stockholders' share value fourfold.*

George Fisher, Chris Galvin, and Gary Tooker

According to Richard C. Buetow, Motorola's senior vice president and director of quality:

> *"For us quality is not a cost, it is a savings."*

Richard C. Buetow

If quality improvement is synonymous with **better, faster** and **lower cost** products and services, how can you **not** get return on investment? A company need not be on the stock market to show return on investment from quality improvement efforts. Consider a few examples:

- Intermedics' Rai Chowdhary began a 4-month quest for quality improvement on the coating of titanium on a cobalt-chrome substrate. The solution to this problem defied all previous medical product expert opinions and approximately 10 years of research from some of the nation's leading material scientists. His efforts in using KISS techniques generated the knowledge to patent the process and save his company from ditching a product which subsequently has generated $60 million of revenue annually.

- Electronic Systems Center at Hanscom AFB, MA, one of three 1994 Quality Improvement Prototype (QIP) Award winners, was able to generate almost a quarter of a million dollar savings annually by applying KISS techniques.

- Walker Parking Consultants, the premier engineering and architectural parking structure firm, has demonstrated continuous process improvement over many years. Their unique approach to scorecard and metric development to measure the quality of their designs has provided them with increased competitiveness for the future.

- Parkview Medical Center in Pueblo, CO, has developed a phenomenal quality improvement culture over the last few years. One success story seems to lead to another. Using KISS techniques to properly categorize clinical pneumonia patients, they have increased yearly revenues by more than $100,000. A spin-off team from the clinical pneumonia team increased the success rate on producing good sputum cultures from a benchmarked 35% to an impressive 95%. Extending the KISS principle to their business practices has allowed them to reduce the accounts receivable process cycle time from 82 days down to 40 days, thereby earning them more than $4 million in interest over a 3½ year period. It seems for Parkview, anyway, that where there's a will, there's a way.

- Lukens Steel's CEO, Bill Van Sant, relates in the October 17, 1995, *USA Today* article "Is TQM Dead?" that quality management techniques have been used not only to cut defects in stainless steel but also to negotiate union contracts.

- Dr. Bert Silich used a designed experiment to amaze the aeronautical design community. He patented a revolutionary aircraft design that numerous experts said would not work.

- A designed experiment was used to develop a Strategic Defense Initiative (SDI) architecture. This effort saved $48 million compared to the proposed method for obtaining the same amount of knowledge.

Numerous other return on investment success stories exist in organizations around the globe. For example, the article "Teaching Top Dogs New Tricks" (*The Boston Globe*, August 22, 1995) relates the plight of two companies and their CEOs who have not only survived, but have prospered in the highly competitive microelectronics industry. Both

Ray Stata and Alexander d'Arbeloff, CEOs of Analog Devices, Inc., and Teradyne, Inc., respectively, credit quality improvement as the key to their staggering increase of more than 60% in quarterly earnings. When asked why he has survived so long and been so successful, Stata replied:

> *"One thing that separates those who hang in is their commitment to continuous learning. What fails some people is their commitment to learn, not their ability."*

Ray Stata

Continuous learning leads to knowledge of customer requirements, products, and processes. As Peter Drucker wrote in the *Atlantic Monthly* (ref. *U.S. News and World Report*, September 11, 1995):

> *"Knowledge has become the key economic resource and the dominant, if not the only, source of comparative advantage."*

Peter Drucker

Francis Bacon, father of the scientific method, stated the following almost 400 years ago:

> *"Knowledge is Power."*

Francis Bacon

The power of knowledge has been clearly demonstrated at General Electric. Jack Welch, the CEO and "America's #1 Manager" according to *Business Week* (June 8, 1998), has implemented a Six Sigma quality initiative which has had phenomenal success. Featured in every major business oriented magazine and newspaper and touted by Wall Street, Welch claims in the *1997 GE Annual Report* the following major successes in just two years:

- GE Medical Systems' new Six Sigma designs have produced a *10-fold* increase in the life of CT scanner x-ray tubes — increasing the "uptime" of these machines and the profitability and level of patient care given by hospitals and other health care providers.

- Superabrasives, GE's industrial diamond business, used Six Sigma to quadruple its return on investment and, by improving yields, is giving it a full *decade's* worth of capacity despite growing volume — without spending a nickel on plant and equipment capacity.

- GE's railcar leasing business has had a 62% reduction in turnaround time at its repair shops — an enormous productivity gain for their railroad and shipper customers and for a business that's now *two to three* times faster than its nearest rival because of Six Sigma improvements. In the next phase, spread across the entire shop network, Black Belts and Green Belts, working with their teams, redesigned the overhaul process, resulting in a *50% further* reduction in cycle time.

- The plastics business, through rigorous Six Sigma process work, added 300 million pounds of new capacity (equivalent to a "free plant"), saved $400 million in investment and will save over another $400 million by the year 2000.

The total savings for GE in 1996 and 1997 is estimated to be over $1 Billion dollars and by the year 2000 projected savings will be over $6 Billion. For more information on Six Sigma, see Appendix D.

The evidence is clear that quality improvement can and will affect the bottom line for those who apply it correctly; and the key to correct application is knowledge. See Figure 2.1.

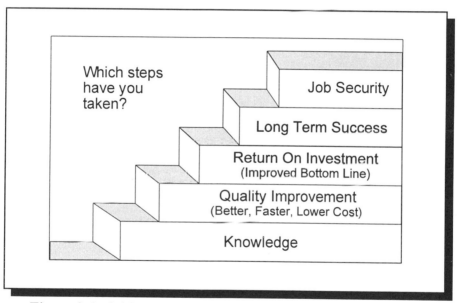

Figure 2.1 Critical KBM Steps to Return On Investment (ROI) and Beyond

What will happen if, on our journey as shown in Figure 2.2, a key step such as knowledge is missing? Companies approaching quality improvement and return on investment without the knowledge step will undoubtedly stumble. At the very least, they will have difficulty changing the organizational culture to achieve long-term success. Maybe this lack of emphasis on knowledge explains why many organizations have yet to start a quality improvement effort or have had false starts, leaving them very disillusioned.

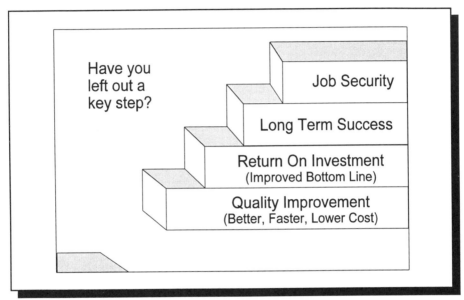

Figure 2.2 Missing Steps Can Cause You to Stumble

Our goal in this text is not only to focus on the philosophies, tools, and techniques, but also to present the material in a way which will help you see the benefits of quality improvement through substantial return on investment (ROI) of time, training, and money. Based on our training and consulting experience, we make every effort to motivate you to eagerly pursue a Knowledge Based Management strategy because we have seen it positively impact the bottom line. The philosophy of how to get started correctly is crucial to obtaining ROI and is the subject of the next chapter.

Chapter 3

PHILOSOPHIES FOR GETTING STARTED

"Deming and I didn't create quality in Japan; all we did was give the Japanese a jump start, a push in the right direction."
J.M. Juran

Most of the quality improvement strategies publicized over the last decade have been based on the philosophies and methods of a select few "quality gurus." Certainly no one can argue with the success of the likes of W. Edwards Deming, J. M. Juran, and K. Ishikawa, who have guided many companies into the quality revolution and on to greater profitability. We firmly believe that regardless of the combination of methods used, the goal for any company should be increased competitiveness (and thus greater chance for survival) through quality improvement of products, services, and associated processes. But how is this achieved? A common but unwritten theme that permeates most of the gurus' philosophies is that enhanced process and product/service knowledge leads to improved quality. But it is a strategy for acquiring that required knowledge base which is missing from many companies' quality endeavors. Which guru do we follow? Just as Tiger Woods would not compete in a championship tournament with just a putter, an iron, or a wood, we, like Tiger, recommend a full bag of clubs (tools) that represents the "best of the best" philosophies, tools and techniques. See Figure 3.1.

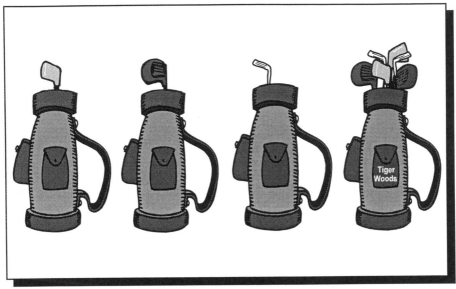

Figure 3.1 Tiger Woods' Bag: A Full Set

In this chapter, we briefly look at some of the ideas from Deming, Juran, and Ishikawa that have steered the quality revolution to its current level. In addition, we develop a philosophy that will make quality management work for you—Knowledge Based Management (KBM). To help you properly manage quality improvement from a "knowledge" standpoint, we will discuss in detail a list of **Questions Managers Need to Answer.** The success of KBM will depend on satisfactorily answering these questions.

The previously mentioned quality gurus would agree that the primary responsibility for quality improvement rests with management. Management sets the goals, cultural climate of the company, its objectives, and its expectations. Management controls the organization's processes, structure, direction, behavioral reward system, values, vision, policies, materials and human resources. If management has not bought into the idea, and if they don't really see the benefits of quality improvement, everything else will usually lead to exercises in frustration and large wastes of time and money. To quote the National Football League (NFL) coaching legend, Sid Gillman,

> *"Quality Control is only as good as your quarterback. If he goes down, you can take your Quality Control and shove it!"*

Sid Gillman

In the days of Sid Gillman, quarterbacks usually were the play callers, i.e., "field managers." A review of NFL history clearly indicates that a team could not get to the superbowl without an outstanding quarterback. Just as the big play maker on most superbowl teams is the quarterback, big plays in industry rest on management's play-calling. Therefore, if a company is going to make a quality improvement sweep around the competition, management must make and execute the call.

Before presenting the list of questions managers need to be able to answer, let's quickly review the philosophies of Deming, Juran, and Ishikawa.

THE DEMING PHILOSOPHY

W. Edwards Deming (1900-1993), physicist, statistician, composer, and world-renowned quality guru, quickly realized that statistical tools, without the management structure to implement the tools, would realize little, if any, return on investment. His management philosophy is captured in Deming's Fourteen Points. These 14 points, which evolved over the years and are based on Deming's experience with both American and Japanese industry, are presented in Table 3.1.

DEMING'S FOURTEEN POINTS

(1)   Create a constancy of purpose toward the improvement of product and service. Consistently aim to improve the design of your products. Innovation, money spent on research and education, and maintenance of equipment will pay off in the long run.

(2)   Adopt a new philosophy of rejecting defective products, poor workmanship, and inattentive service. Defective items are a terrible drain on a company; the total cost to produce and dispose of a defective item exceeds the cost to produce a good one, and defective items do not generate revenues.

(Continued on next page)

Table 3.1 Deming's Fourteen Points

(3)   Do not depend on mass inspection because it is usually too late, too costly, and ineffective. Realize that quality does not come from inspection, but from improvements on the process.

(4)   Do not award business on price tag alone, but consider quality as well. Price is only a meaningful criterion if it is set in relation to a measure of quality. The strategy of awarding work to the lowest bidder has the tendency to drive good vendors and good service out of business. Preference should be given to reliable suppliers that use modern methods of statistical quality control to assess the quality of their production.

(5)   Constantly improve the system of production and service. Involve workers in this process, but also use statistical experts who can separate special causes of poor quality from common ones.

(6)   Institute modern training methods. Instructions to employees must be clear and precise. Workers should be well trained.

(7)   Institute modern methods of supervision. Supervision should not be viewed as passive "surveillance," but as active participation aimed at helping the employee make a better product.

(Continued on next page)

Table 3.1 Deming's Fourteen Points

(8)   Drive out fear. Great economic loss is usually associated with fear when workers are afraid to ask a question or to take a position. A secure worker will report equipment out of order, will ask for clarifying instructions, and will point to conditions that impair quality and production.

(9)   Break down the barriers between functional areas. Teamwork among the different departments is needed.

(10)   Eliminate numerical goals for your work force. Eliminate targets and slogans. Setting the goals for other people without providing a plan on how to reach these goals is often counterproductive. It is far better to explain what management is doing to improve the system.

(11)   Eliminate work standards and numerical quotas. Work standards are usually without reference to produced quality. Work standards, piece work, and quotas are manifestations of the inability to understand and provide supervision. Quality must be built in.

(12)   Remove barriers that discourage the hourly worker from doing his or her job. Management should listen to hourly workers and try to understand their complaints, comments, and suggestions. Management should treat their workers as important participants in the production process and not as opponents across a bargaining table.

(Continued on next page)

Table 3.1 Deming's Fourteen Points

(13) Institute a vigorous program of training and education. Education in simple, but powerful, statistical techniques should be required of all employees. Statistical quality control charts should be made routinely and they should be displayed in a place where everyone can see them. Such charts document the quality of a process over time. Employees who are aware of the current level of quality are more likely to investigate the reasons for poor quality and find ways of improving the process. Ultimately, such investigations result in better products.

(14) Create a structure in top management that will vigorously advocate these 13 points.

Table 3.1 Deming's Fourteen Points

Source: Deming, W.E., Out of the Crisis, MIT Center for Advanced Engineering Study, Cambridge, MA, (1982).

"Sound understanding of statistical control is essential to management, engineering, manufacturing, purchase of materials, and service."

W. Edwards Deming

THE JURAN PHILOSOPHY

Like Deming, Joseph M. Juran spent a good bit of time in Japan during the early 1950's. Juran developed his philosophy and approach over many years, and in 1979, he founded the Juran Institute to provide training and consulting to those wanting to pursue quality improvement. Table 3.2 presents his ten practical steps to quality improvement.

JURAN'S 10 STEPS

1. Build awareness of the need and opportunity for improvement.

2. Set goals for improvement.

3. Organize to reach the goals (have a plan and an organizational structure).

4. Provide training.

5. Carry out projects to solve problems.

(Continued on next page)

Table 3.2 J. M. Juran's 10 Steps to Quality Improvement

6. Report progress.

7. Give recognition.

8. Communicate results.

9. Keep score.

10. Maintain momentum by making annual improvement part of the regular systems and process of the organization.

Table 3.2 J. M. Juran's 10 Steps to Quality Improvement

Source: J.M. Juran, Juran on Planning for Quality.
The Free Press, New York 1988.

"Product and service quality requires managerial, technological, and statistical concepts throughout all the major functions in an organization."

J.M. Juran

THE ISHIKAWA PHILOSOPHY

Kaoru Ishikawa, a Japanese engineer with noted accomplishments in the quality arena, sees Quality Improvement (he referred to it as Quality Control) as a thought revolution in management. He has developed a list of things that top management must do. We present this list in an abbreviated form. See Table 3.3.

ISHIKAWA: WHAT MUST TOP MANAGEMENT DO?

- Study quality improvement ahead of anyone else in your company and understand the issues involved.

- Establish the policies towards promoting quality improvement efforts—what the general attitudes will be.

- Specify the priorities for implementing quality improvement and the short and long term goals.

- Assume a leadership role in making quality improvement happen.

- Provide a means for educating the people.

- Check to see if quality improvement is implemented as planned.

(Continued on next page)

Table 3.3 K. Ishikawa's List of Things Top Management Must Do

- Make clear the responsibility of top management.

- Establish a system of cross functional management.

- Drive home the notion that the outputs from your process are inputs to your customers.

- Provide leadership towards making a "breakthrough" happen.

Table 3.3 K. Ishikawa's List of Things Top Management Must Do

Source: K. Ishikawa, <u>What is Total Quality Control?</u>
Prentice Hall, Engelwood Cliffs, N.J. 1985.

THE KNOWLEDGE BASED MANAGEMENT PHILOSOPHY

The three previous quality improvement philosophies have captured a significant following with much success. Yet many managers see these philosophies as emphasizing the "what" of quality improvement, and they struggle with "how" to make it happen. Knowledge Based Management (KBM) is an extension of the works of Deming, Juran, and Ishikawa with a focus on the "hows."

Deming frequently used the term "profound knowledge." We believe that profound knowledge implies the ability to answer profound questions. Therefore, the guiding principles of KBM are centered around a set of specific Questions Managers Need to Answer. See Table 3.4.

Managers should test themselves on these questions before reading beyond Table 3.4. Correctly answering these questions will lay the ground work for successfully implementing quality improvement.

**QUALITY IMPROVEMENT ORIENTED
QUESTIONS MANAGERS NEED TO ANSWER!**

1. What is your product or service and who are your customers?

2. What perception do your customers have of your product or service? How do you know?

3. Do you believe quality issues are important to your company? Why? Which ones?

4. What is the company's current share of the total market? Can quality improvement efforts assist you in increasing the market share and/or increasing profits? How?

5. Are you actively pursuing quality improvement in your areas of responsibility? How?

6. How many hours (days) per week (month) do you currently have scheduled (on your calendar) that are devoted strictly to quality issues?

7. How often per week (month) do you solicit feedback from the people you manage? What kind of feedback do you solicit? What do you do with the feedback?

(Continued on next page)

Table 3.4 Quality Improvement Oriented Questions
Managers Need to Answer!

8. What are the right quality-oriented questions managers need to ask their people? What methods or tools can be used to answer them?

9. Are your people trained to successfully use the best quality improvement tools? What is your Return On Investment (ROI) from the training?

10. Do you have a standard procedure for documenting quality improvement efforts? What is it?

11. What barriers do your people face when trying to do quality improvement? What are you doing to remove these barriers?

12. What metrics are you evaluated on that relate to quality issues? Are you held accountable for these metrics? What are the specific improvement goals for these metrics?

13. How much waste does your company have? That is, what (in dollars) is the company's Cost Of Poor Quality (COPQ)? How much of the total waste is your area responsible for?

14. One year from now what evidence will you have to show that you made a difference?

Table 3.4 Quality Improvement Oriented Questions
Managers Need to Answer!

How the top-level and mid-level managers answer these questions is crucial to the long term success of any company. In the following pages we discuss each question at length.

QUALITY IMPROVEMENT ORIENTED QUESTIONS MANAGERS NEED TO ANSWER!

> 1. **What is your product or service and who are your customers?**

Obviously, a manager needs to thoroughly understand what his/her company is all about. Very specific information is required to successfully answer this question. Mission and Vision statements that clearly address the company's purpose can aid in this understanding.

Mission/Vision Statements

Many quality improvement concepts are common sense. Mission and Vision statements fall into this category. It seems that any company should know why it is in business and where it is going. In fact, perhaps the best mission statement is "to make a profit." After all, this is why any company (excluding some non-profit organizations) is in business. Let's face it; if the company doesn't make money, it closes its doors. However, the Mission statement should go well beyond "making a profit." It should explain how the company plans to stay in business, what the primary product/service is, and how that product/service relates to the marketplace.

One weakness in developing Mission and Vision statements is that the company may spend months on making sure that exactly the right words are in the statement and making sure that everyone involved in the drafting of the statement is happy with the final product. In the meantime, little else gets done in the area of quality improvement because senior leadership is so wrapped up in writing Mission statements. We don't have to make it that complicated.

In writing the Mission statement, ask yourself:

1. *What do we produce and/or what service do we provide?*

2. *What characteristics of this product/service make it a valuable commodity to our customers?*

In writing the Vision statement, ask:

1. *How are we going to ensure that we can compete in the future?*

2. *What things, specifically, do we need to do in order to lead the competition in our industry?*

Mission and Vision statements are not meant to be complex expositions that lay out a ten-year plan for production and explain how it will be accomplished. They should:

- *be short and concise,*

- *tell what we do (Mission) and where we are going (Vision),*

-    *be measured by how well they are communicated to the employees and customers and by the level of commitment by senior leadership. Climate surveys are a means of measuring this communication and commitment. It is interesting to note that some of the best books on Vision and Mission statements are actually books on leadership!*

Example:

Our company, Air Academy Press & Associates, is a company that trains and consults in the area of quality improvement. We specialize in the tools (many of which are statistical in nature) that are used in quality improvement.

In developing our Mission Statement, we would ask:

1.   *What do we produce and/or what service do we provide?*

Our products are textbooks, software and training aids aimed at quality improvement. Our services are training and consultation on the use of quality improvement tools.

2.   *What characteristics of this product/service make it a valuable commodity to our customers?*

Through training and exposure to the correct and efficient use of quality improvement tools, our customers will gain knowledge of their products/services and processes. This will result in

return on investment through reduced waste, reduced cycle time and improved performance that will further lead to their becoming leaders in their respective industries.

Our resulting Mission Statement is given below:

We believe that only through continued learning and the application of proven methodologies can today's companies gain the knowledge required to sustain leading positions in world technology, production, and service.

Our goal is to provide the tools to accomplish this task.

Without a clear understanding of your organization's Mission and Vision statements, any further efforts will lack direction.

"Where there is no vision, the people perish."

Prov 29:18

> 2. What perception do your customers have of your product or service? How do you know?

Managers should have easy access to the data from customers' surveys. They should be able to show how they collected the customer information and the data that led to their conclusion.

We expect managers to share their opinions, but it is important that these opinions are backed by facts and data that represent the customers' perception. The answer to this question gives you a good clue as to where you are and how seriously you need to take future quality improvement efforts. Also keep in mind that even an excellent customer perception today can be gone tomorrow with the emergence of new competitors or new technologies. We can never get complacent just because customers are happy today.

Are companies today really customer oriented? According to Mr. Curtis Riemann of the National Institute of Standards and Technology,

> *"Early quality improvements sometimes had nothing to do with the company's key businesses. Baldrige applicants were obviously reporting things they had improved rather than things that were crucial to the customers."*

Curtis Riemann

---

3. Do you believe quality issues are important to your company? Why? Which ones?

The intent of this question is to see if the manager understands the entire spectrum of quality improvement issues. It will also expose those who simply give quality improvement "lip service." For example, if a manager answers "yes" to part one but cannot explain why or which ones, then he/she doesn't really believe in quality.

Various quality issues should be discussed. A quality issue is anything that will enable us to make our product or service **better, faster** *and at a* **lower cost.** *For example, defect rate, yield, variation, C_{pk}, cycle time, product/process development time, start-up time, cost of poor quality, waste, price, customer satisfaction, profits, reliability, safety, environmental impact, etc., are some of the more common quality measures used today.*

The quality issues that are important to an organization drive the key quality metrics (measurement variables) by which that organization measures quality performance. Our research has shown that companies which place as much emphasis on key quality improvement measurements as they do on other key business and financial metrics are the companies that get an excellent ROI on their quality improvement effort.

> **4. What is the company's current share of the total market? Can quality improvement efforts assist you in increasing the market share and/or increasing profits?**

It is crucial that managers understand and believe deep down in their hearts that quality improvement (if done correctly) will have a substantial impact on the bottom line. It is sad that many companies who currently experience large annual growth don't feel the need to embrace quality improvement until next year's projection levels out or declines. Whether your company is in a high growth mode or not, quality improvement will help optimize the bottom line results. Managers must not only believe this but also be "on fire" rather than "lukewarm" about implementation. It is unfortunate that many companies do not embrace quality improvement until they are on their death beds. By then, the seeds of destruction may be too well germinated to reverse the lethal trend. That is why we must continuously target and plan our quality improvement efforts. Anything less will lead to increased levels of frustration and confusion and possibly failure.

> *"Quality now is like oxygen.*
> *It's not optional."*

B. Joseph White
Dean of the University of Michigan Business School

5. Are you actively pursuing quality improvement in your areas of responsibility? How?

If a manager has answered questions 1 through 4 satisfactorily but yet cannot give specific examples of how quality improvement has been successfully implemented, the "lips" and the "heart" are not saying the same thing. See Figure 3.2.

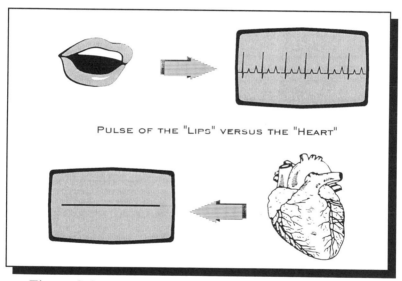

PULSE OF THE "LIPS" VERSUS THE "HEART"

Figure 3.2 Do the Lips Reflect the True Nature of the
Heart When it Comes to Commitment to Quality?

Active pursuit of quality improvement is more than talking about or even initiating a quality improvement program. It involves management participation, support, and commitment, as well as training. When we get to question 8 we will suggest a strategy of "questions managers need to ask" which will help you get started.

> **6.** **How many hours (days) per week (month) do you currently have scheduled (on your calendar) that are devoted strictly to quality issues?**

Managers who have strong convictions about quality improvement will naturally integrate the time into their daily activities. Others may need to have specific time entered in their schedule until it becomes a natural part of how they do business.

> **"If it's not scheduled on the boss's calendar it's not getting done!"**

Jan Gaudin

Managers need to know not only where and with which activities they spend their time but also where the people they supervise spend their time. Pareto charts and Pareto analyses of time spent are valuable tools for process improvement because Cost Of Poor Quality (COPQ) is usually correlated to those activities with high time utilization. See the following two graphs in Figure 3.3 taken from the article "Does TQM Have Return on Investment—If Not, Why Not" by Schmidt, Cheek, and Kiemele.

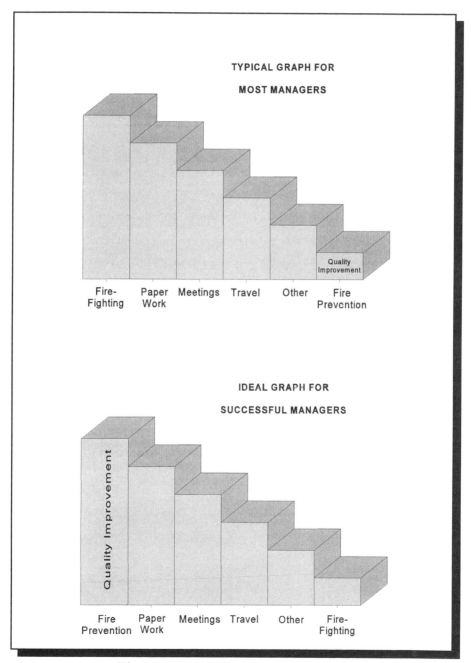

Figure 3.3 Utilizing Time Effectively

> **7. How often per week (month) do you solicit feedback
> from the people you manage? What kind of feedback
> do you solicit? What do you do with the feedback?**

*Although managers have the responsibility for successfully
implementing quality improvement, the best ideas of how to do
it are often in the minds of those who deal with the job details
on a daily basis. Enlighten your employees that their job
security is directly tied to how competitive the company is, and
they will be volunteering to give you feedback on what should
be done. Make sure you are ready to listen and willing to
implement the good ideas. What is the status of your company's
suggestion (or ideas) program? This is a valuable source of
information and, if used properly, can be an important
motivational factor for employees.*

*Another important avenue for gaining useful information is
to evaluate the climate within the company. A simple list of
well-thought out questions can be used to obtain feedback on
the attitudes and presumptions of all employees. Employees
must always be kept in the loop with regard to the results of an
organizational survey and if any action is being taken as a
result of the survey.*

*The bottom line is not to let your organizational chart resemble
the one shown in Figure 3.4.*

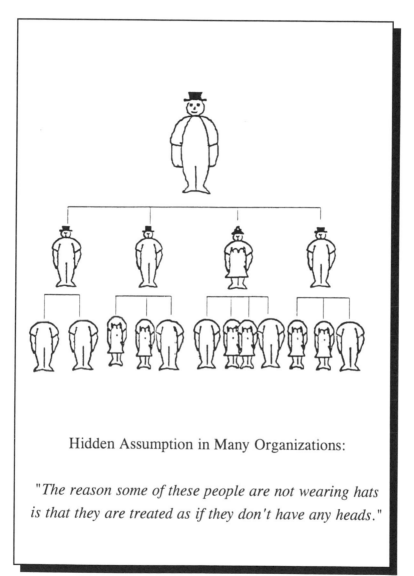

Hidden Assumption in Many Organizations:

*"The reason some of these people are not wearing hats
is that they are treated as if they don't have any heads."*

Figure 3.4 Don't Let Your Organizational
Chart Look Like This!

Source: Quality First, Dr. Myron Tribus

> **8. What are the right quality oriented questions managers need to ask? What methods or tools can be used to answer them?**

Our experience indicates that many managers don't know the right questions to ask. In fact, some managers are often intimidated by their lack of process knowledge. However, a generic set of questions will empower most managers to find out the professional knowledge level of their employees. The next set of questions is recommended for managers who want to find what the corporate knowledge level is for a given activity (process, product, or service oriented). Obviously, every activity will not require that all 14 questions be answered.

**QUALITY IMPROVEMENT ORIENTED QUESTIONS
MANAGERS NEED TO ASK THEIR PEOPLE!**

1. What processes (activities) are you responsible for? Who is the owner of those processes? Who are the team members?

2. Which processes have the highest priority for improvement? How did you come to this conclusion? Where is the data that led to this conclusion?

(Continued on next page)

Table 3.5 Quality Improvement Oriented Questions
Managers Need to Ask Their People

For those processes to be improved,

3. How is the process performed?

4. What are your process performance measures? Why? How accurate and precise is your measurement system?

5. What are the customer-driven specifications for all of your performance measures? How good or bad is the current performance? Show me the data. What are the improvement goals for the process?

6. What are all the sources of variability in the process? Show me what they are.

7. Which sources of variability do you control? How do you control them and what is your method of documentation?

8. Are any of the sources of variability supplier-dependent? If so, what are they, who is the supplier, and what are we doing about it?

(Continued on next page)

Table 3.5 Quality Improvement Oriented Questions Managers Need to Ask Their People

9. What are the key variables that affect the average and variation of the measures of performance? How do you know this? Show me the data.

10. What are the relationships between the measures of performance and the key variables? Do any key variables interact? How do you know for sure? Show me the data.

11. What setting for each of the key variables will optimize the measures of performance? How do you know this? Show me the data.

12. For the optimal settings of the key variables, what kind of variability exists in the performance measures? Is it too large? How do you know? Show me the data.

13. How much improvement has the process shown in the past six months? How do you know this? Show me the data.

14. How much time and/or money have your efforts saved or generated for the company? How did you document all of your efforts? Show me the data.

Table 3.5 Quality Improvement Oriented Questions Managers Need to Ask Their People

> *"If managers don't know the right questions to ask, how will employees ever know if they have any of the right answers?"*

Anonymous

Knowing the right questions to ask is one thing, but we also need to know the most powerful tools available to get answers. Just as we would not tolerate an engineer in the 1990's using a slide rule for mathematical calculations, or a secretary using an ordinary typewriter to type a letter, we should not allow scientists and engineers and employees in general to use antiquated problem solving techniques. Therefore, it is extremely important that managers not only know the right questions to ask but also are familiar with the best tools to be used to answer these questions. When a manager sends someone to training there should be an expectation of how that person will utilize the training back on the job.

In order to address today's complex problems, the next three chapters will expand on each of the questions in Table 3.5 and provide the tools and techniques to answer them. This type of knowledge is a minimum for a manager to successfully implement quality improvement in his/her area.

> **9. Are your people trained to successfully use the best quality improvement tools? What is your Return On Investment (ROI) from the training?**

*The key part of this question is return on investment. A "Quality Observer" article (May 1994) by Schmidt, Cheek, and Kiemele entitled "**Does TQM Have Return On Investment—If Not, Why Not?**" depicts a structured training implementation approach which has been proven to lead to substantial return on investment. See Figure 3.5 on the following page. Training alone will only produce "knowers." Therefore, more than training is required to get return on investment. Motorola and Texas Instruments have had great success in promoting "Black Belt" programs, wherein a "black belt" is a key person identified as a quality improvement champion or "doer." The purpose of a "black belt" is to be a catalyst in making application of the training come to life. Obviously, every new black belt is not fully competent and/or confident in a wide variety of complex programs. Consequently, a "mentor" program is also instituted where the mentor acts as a coach or "helper" to assist black belts and oversee their progress. The key to the entire structure, however, is accountability for training black belts and mentors. This accountability can only be achieved if each person is evaluated on the proper metrics (measurement variables). The development of these metrics should produce a scorecard much like the one shown in Table 3.6 which is*

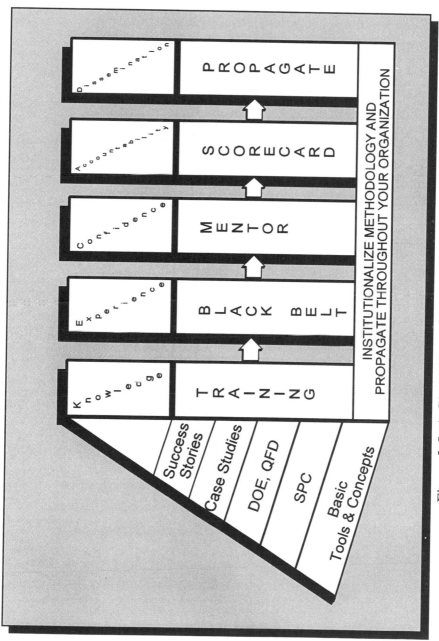

Figure 3.5 A Global Strategy to Achieve Training ROI

used to answer Question 12. The final tier in Figure 3.5 is then to propagate or disseminate the success stories and the methodology that was used to generate them.

	Performance	Schedule	Cost
Organization			
Product			
Process			
People			

Table 3.6 A Scorecard Worksheet for Metric Development

*The strategy depicted in Figure 3.5 to achieve ROI from training is designed to get at the heart of the training evaluation issue. Kirkpatrick (Training, March 1995) developed a 4-level model that can be used to evaluate training. The lowest (and easiest to measure) level of Kirkpatrick's model is to answer the question "Did the students **like** the training?" While many dismiss this level as trivial and not really telling us if the training actually worked, it is far from meaningless because if a student does not perceive the training to be applicable to the job, it probably won't be. The second level of his model addresses the question of "Did the students **learn** the material they were taught?" Although not as easy to measure as the first level, Level 2 is measurable. The* *third level in the Kirkpatrick model has to do with "Do the (now former) students **use** the training they received?" The highest level, and certainly the most difficult to measure, is to determine "What is the **return on investment (ROI)** from our training dollars?" To achieve evaluation of training at this highest level will require an organizational support structure such as the one shown in Figure 3.5 and a company wide emphasis on Cost Of Poor Quality. The Six Sigma Project Master Strategy described in Appendix D is designed precisely for the purpose of generating ROI.*

> "The price of gaining knowledge is nothing compared to the cost of ignorance."

Anonymous

As a final note, training and applications must be seen as a bottom line generating asset and not as a liability. As such, we should think carefully before reducing training budgets too much during hard times.

According to the CEO at Lukens Steel, Mr. Bill Van Sant, quoted in USA Today's article "Is TQM Dead?", October 17, 1995,

> "Quality management has got to be championed in good times and bad. Often, it rises and falls based on the status of the company."

Bill Van Sant

---

10. Do you have a standard procedure for documenting quality improvement efforts? What is it?

It is alarming that most employees in industry are not given a notebook containing all the accumulated knowledge for the processes they are responsible for. That means that any prior knowledge gained was lost when the employee took over the new job. In this situation any new employee has to start over gathering knowledge—a very expensive practice. This scenario is exacerbated for companies with high turnover rates. Gaining knowledge is important, but without good documentation and communication we will continually "re-invent the wheel." In today's competitive marketplace, business units—whether they be in government, industry, or academia—do not have this luxury. Resources—people, time, and money—are limited. In order to gain ROI, we will have to do more with less.

Furthermore, many mandated quality improvement efforts such as ISO-9000 (international quality standard), QS-9000 (automotive industry standard), D1-9000 (Boeing supplier standard), Quality Systems Review (QSR, Motorola standard), Process Characterization (electronics industry standard), and Process Validation (FDA regulatory standard for pharmaceuticals and medical devices) are simply a repackaging of what should have already been documented in an activity notebook.

> **11. What barriers do your people face when trying to do quality improvement? What are you doing to remove these barriers?**

If managers don't know the barriers their people face, how can they lead their employees to success? Table 3.7 depicts the results of a survey of more than 1000 of our class participants who came from a variety of work environments. The individual responses have been grouped into seven major categories so we can better focus on how to remove those barriers. We suspect these barriers show up to some extent in almost every organization. How many of these barriers exist in your organization, and what are you doing to remove them?

Consider the last barrier listed under attitude and motivation: **lack the will to win***. If we lack the will to win, then losing will be a self-fulfilling prophecy. Also consider this: if we truly have the will to win, nothing short of death will stop us from moving forward.*

> *"Not to know is bad;*
> *not to wish to know is worse."*

African Proverb

BARRIERS TO QUALITY IMPROVEMENT

Management	Time	Communications
• Lack of leadership	• Too busy firefighting	• Poor documentation
• Few role models	• People are weary from long hours	• Culture not right for sharing knowledge
• Unclear direction	• Improper time management	• Poor knowledge of customer needs
• Not willing to increase emphasis on gaining complete knowledge in R&D and design	• Duplicated effort	• Don't let suppliers know how to help us
• Not willing or knowledgeable to ask the right questions	• Too many arguments without facts and data	• Inability to properly present something
• Does not encourage enough time to plan	• Perception that new tools take too much time	• Communicate to managers with emotion instead of facts, data and dollars
• Too many layers	• Too many unproductive meetings	• Conflicting messages
• Wants immediate results versus substantial growth in knowledge through use of scientific method	• Timeline pressure	• Information politics
• Don't track the right metrics	• Too busy reorganizing	• Tools for properly communicating process information not known or used
• Ignorant of the new tools for success		
• Not focused on knowledge gained per resource per unit time		
• Continued emphasis on old ways of doing business		
• Reluctant to support new methods		
• Inadequate emphasis on waste (COPQ) identification and reduction		(Continued on next page)

Table 3.7 Barriers to Quality Improvement

Training	Resources	Reward System	Attitude and Motivation
• Not enough people properly trained	• Limited resources	• Promotes firefighting	• Laziness
• Inability to think and use common sense	• Insufficient manpower	• Supports traditional power centers	• Don't perceive problems as threatening
• Some people need a refresher course	• Insufficient internal experts to assist others	• People not held accountable	• Rush to get results without planning
• Management last to be trained versus first	• Inadequate or inappropriate use of outside consultants	• People (groups) compete against each other versus helping	• Easier to blame others than to take responsibility
• Need more motivation in training of basic tools	• Improper allocation of resources	• Perception that powerful tools will uncover poor decisions	• Critical and/or negative attitudes
• Need for a mentor program		• No consequences for not implementing continuous improvement	• Resistance to change
• Need for follow-up assistance			• Professional firefighters feel threatened
• Suppliers need to be trained			• New concepts take time
• Not enough emphasis on COPQ, how to identify it and reduce it			• Fear of failure using new methods
• Unqualified trainers			• Fear of downsizing
• Training is not JIT			• Unwilling to share what you know with others
• Lack of funding			• Lack the "will to win"
• Not enough emphasis on ROI			

Table 3.7 Barriers to Quality Improvement

> **12. What metrics are you evaluated on that relate to quality issues? Are you held accountable for these metrics? What are the specific improvement goals for these metrics?**

Metrics are nothing more than specific measures that one can accumulate, teach, and evaluate. The posting of these metrics and how we use them to hold management accountable will to a large degree define your company's culture. As Vince Lombardi said,

> **"If you are not keeping score, you are just practicing."**

Vince Lombardi

*Thus, keeping score drives the strategy of the game, and careful consideration must be given as to what the **proper** metrics to be posted really should be. For example, in football the scoreboard reflects the number of points scored by each team. Imagine the strategy of the game if, instead of number of points, we posted only the number of first downs! That is, number of first downs determined whether we won or lost. We could radically change the playing strategy overnight by posting a different scorecard. The long pass, punts and field goals would disappear. The game would be more of a series of four downs for ten yard efforts.*

The same thing is true in industry. If the score only reflects products shipped, services rendered, timelines, and budgets, you will rarely get ROI from quality improvement. See Figure 3.6. If you want reduced COPQ, cycle time, number of changes, number of defects, number of customer complaints, etc., you will need to post it, track it and hold management accountable. Without the proper scorecard, management will keep us practicing for quality improvement but we will never get into the real game. Use Table 3.8 as a guideline and worksheet to seek out metrics in all vital areas.

To use the table, place current metrics in the appropriate box or use the matrix to brainstorm new metrics. For example, a performance metric for the total organization might be market share. A scheduling metric might be timeliness or on time delivery. A cost metric might be operational cost. See Table 7.1 in Chapter 7 for a completed example.

	Performance	Schedule	Cost
Organization			
Product			
Process			
People			

Table 3.8 A Scorecard Worksheet for Metric Development

Figure 3.6 Example of an Incomplete Scorecard.
What Scorecard is Your Company Playing To?
Is It the Right Scorecard?

We not only need to develop the right metrics but we must also implement a strategy to hold managers accountable for these metrics. Note that the scorecard system will drive the organization in a specific direction. This powerful tool should not be implemented without careful thought. It is also worth noting that once we decide on our scorecard and how to track it, we need to ensure that everyone keeps accurate data!

Another key issue related to metrics is the improvement rate goal. In the April 1994 issue of Quality Progress, *an article titled "Improving the Odds of TQM's Success" by Loyd Eskildson cited inadequate goals as a major reason for failed TQM programs. He mentioned that "Motorola, Harley-Davidson, Hewlett Packard, Xerox, and others initiated their quality transformation with dramatic, challenging goals for the short term and attained impressive results." He states that to improve the odds of success, we must "establish demanding, customer-focused improvement goals."*

In our experience many organizations have no goals for their improvement metrics. If they do have goals, then they are often either not challenging enough, such as 10% improvement per year, or else they are a flat goal such as 95% on time delivery. The problem with flat goals is that once they are met there is no motivation to go beyond. The way Motorola addressed this was to set a goal of 10 fold reduction in defect levels every two years. This is how they achieved the 200 fold reduction in defect levels quoted earlier. The effect that aggressive goal setting had was to actually drive a culture change. In this case the change was to adopt a mindset for finding different and better ways to do things in order to meet the improvement goal. Motorola also had a goal to reduce cycle time by a factor of 10 every five years. In other words, if the time from when an order is placed until it is shipped is now twenty days, five years from now the time from placement to shipping should be two days.

In order to meet aggressive goals it takes commitment from all levels of the organization, but the goals are crucial. Every measurement chart should have a goal line on it to determine if the improvement rate goals are met. See Figures 3.7a and 3.7b for a graphic depicting Motorola's aggressive (stretch) goals.

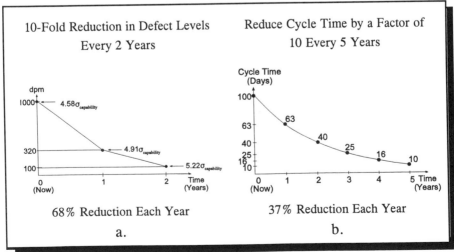

Figure 3.7 Motorola's Stretch Goals

13. How much waste does your company have? That is, what (in dollars) is the company's Cost Of Poor Quality (COPQ)? How much of the total waste is your area responsible for?

*Most companies, managers, and employees are not able to quantify the Cost Of Poor Quality (COPQ) in their area because they have not identified the **sources** of waste, scrap, and rework. And those that have estimated their COPQ seldom have a realistic value based on all areas of waste. If you don't know where you are today, how can you estimate how much you've saved tomorrow (i.e., what is your return on investment)?*

"About one-third of what we do in this country consists of redoing what we did before. Chronic waste is enormous. Defects are like alligators and we're up to our hips in alligators. We keep shooting them, and they keep coming back. Why? Because we aren't planning properly. All we do is plan ways to shoot the alligators. We need to plan so we can eliminate them altogether."

J.M. Juran

Let's look at a picture of what has been happening in companies across the United States. Consider Figure 3.8a where the price of any product or service is driven by profits and total cost to produce or provide.

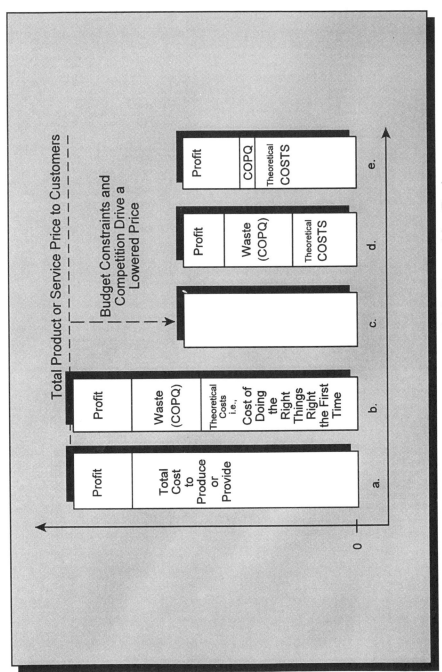

Figure 3.8 Maintaining Profits in Highly Competitive Environments

In Figure 3.8b we see that the total cost to produce can be broken into two categories: (1) cost associated with doing the right things right the first time and (2) waste or non-value added costs, sometimes referred to as the Cost of Poor Quality or COPQ. According to quality gurus such as Deming, Juran, etc., the percentage of COPQ in most companies is 20-40% of the total sales. Now consider Figure 3.8c where a competitor or customer-driven fixed cost or possibly budget cuts have mandated a lower price. The company represented by Figure 3.8d has responded to the new lowered price by laying off one half of its work force and/or selling off non-profitable assets, but it has done very little to cut the COPQ. This response is typical of most U.S. managed companies as seen on the news or read about in newspapers over the last 4 to 5 years. The company that will survive global markets in the 1990's and on into the twenty-first century is depicted in Figure 3.8e. It has attacked and cut its COPQ significantly. The key to competitiveness and survival is tied to reducing the 20% to 40% waste due to poor quality, high cycle times, long development times, non-value added activities, high defect rates (or low yields), excessive inventories, duplicated efforts, transfer problems, changes, poorly optimized processes, etc. The latter approach is more difficult in the short term, but it is the only way to long-term profitability and competitiveness.

> **14. One year from now what evidence will you have to show that you made a difference?**

If we don't have a plan to measure our impact on the company's bottom line, our apathy projects a "will to lose" which will be a self-fulfilling prophecy. For most readers of this text, our job security is in our own hands. We can and must make a difference. So that we don't overestimate or underestimate our worth to the company, plan on developing a way to measure our impact on the company's bottom line.

As a final note, be committed to play the game forever! Don't give up or give in even when it gets frustrating. What are our alternatives? Consider a statement from Fred Schmidt, the CEO of FedEx,

> *"It is easy to get frustrated. Quality management is very hard to do. It takes a long time and constant reiteration and every possible kind of management effort to keep it on track."*

Fred Schmidt

For an overview of how Jack Welch (CEO at General Electric) has managed to keep a Six Sigma quality effort on track using a Knowledge Based Management (KBM) approach, see Appendix D.

Chapter 4

IMPLEMENTATION STRATEGIES

"Every prudent man acts out of knowledge..."

Prov 13:16

Better, Faster, and Lower Cost Products and Services are not something that just happens! We must have a plan or strategy for finding the opportunities for improvement, implementing the change, and following up. These strategies are the roadmap to increased quality, market share, and profitability. Common sense suggests a balanced approach to implementing organizational, product, service, process and people quality improvements. The organization is obviously concerned with short-term, as well as long-term, effects on the bottom line. Therefore, any quality improvement strategy must be robust enough to meet both needs. We cannot be so naive as to suggest that long-term quality improvement of products, services and processes is the only focus. If we don't ship product or perform service in the short-term, there will be no short-term bottom line and perhaps no long-term bottom line either.

> "*Achieving quality is not a guarantee of success. In the early 1980's, People's Express, the first no-frills, low price airline, practiced tenets of TQM. It was customer-focused, and it empowered workers by rotating jobs. But the airline went under when it tried to horn in on major airlines' routes. They failed Marketing 101. They failed Competitive Strategy 101.*"

B. Joseph White
Dean of the University of Michigan Business School

Previous chapters have presented a philosophy for long-term quality improvement. This is the "what" of Knowledge Based Management (KBM). Now we need to look at the "how." Realizing the need to meet short-term requirements, we present this chapter as a guide for implementing quality improvement wherever opportunities exist. It provides a strategy for identifying areas of improvement and gaining proper knowledge to make the improvements that will realize gains for the organization. This chapter lists tools that can be used to make successful improvements, and subsequent chapters will outline those tools in more detail.

Actual product and service quality have often been de-emphasized in light of the big push for process quality. In reality we need them all. Product and service quality are especially important early in the development and design phases. This is verified in a special report published in a 1987 *Business Week* magazine indicating that 20% to 50% of most companies' operating budget is allocated to identifying and fixing mistakes. It also suggests that as many as one-fourth of all manpower requirements are assigned to these tasks. Furthermore, as much as 80% of all quality defects result because of failing to understand customer requirements. Software quality is a specific case in point (see Figure 4.1).

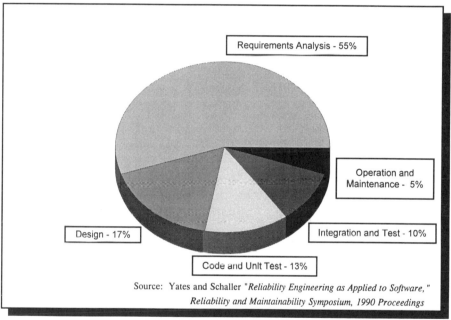

Figure 4.1 Percentage of Software Errors that Originate
in Each Phase of the Software Development Lifecycle

To determine our customers' needs and expectations requires that we ask them and then be willing to listen to their answer(s). It is also important to patiently assist the customers because they often do not fully understand their needs. The importance of correctly addressing customer needs was pointed out by W.D. Yates and D.A. Schaller, in their presentation *"Reliability Engineering as Applied to Software,"* at the 1990 Reliability and Maintainability Symposium.

> *"The requirements analysis phase is the biggest contributor to errors in the development cycle."*

Yates and Schaller, 1990

Figure 4.1 also indicates that the design phase is the second largest contributor to errors. With 72% of software development errors originating in requirements analysis and design, the obvious area to be emphasized for improved quality is at the beginning of the development cycle. A clear understanding of customer requirements will prevent numerous change proposals. Each change not only increases development time but also increases the chance for new errors and higher costs. As you would expect, the cost for correcting errors will increase dramatically as the point of error detection moves downstream in the development cycle. Therefore, early error detection and prevention is vitally important.

Strategies to gain knowledge in product and service development and design are centered around a Japanese approach referred to as Quality Function Deployment (QFD). QFD is both a strategy and a tool which provides a mechanism for multi-functional teams to capture the knowledge of all aspects of customer requirements and to translate these requirements into product/service development and design. A global view of QFD is depicted in Figure 4.2. At this point we only refer to QFD as a strategy to obtain knowledge of product and service quality as early in the development cycle as possible. More information on QFD as a tool is presented in later chapters.

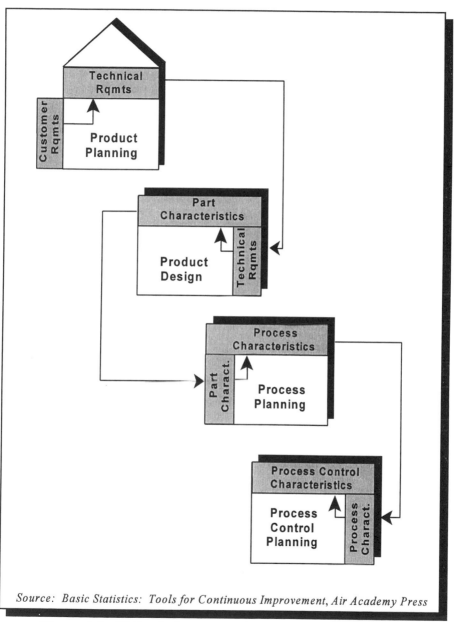

Source: *Basic Statistics: Tools for Continuous Improvement, Air Academy Press*

Figure 4.2 QFD: A Structured Approach Used to Capture
Customer Requirements and Map Them Into
Development, Design, and Process Requirements

Quality improvement early on is critical to reducing cycle times, defect rates, and cost of poor quality (COPQ). To implement a QFD strategy implies that we are attempting to be customer focused. This also implies that we are willing to ask the customers for inputs and then listen to their responses. Lam, Watson, and Schmidt in *Total Quality: A Textbook of Strategic Quality, Leadership and Planning* list nine reasons companies have difficulty committing to customer focus.

NINE REASONS WE STRUGGLE WITH A COMMITTED CUSTOMER FOCUS

1. We like to believe we know what customers want better than they do. The approach of American business has often been to develop products/services and then convince customers they want them, through slick marketing techniques.

2. An arm's length relationship has existed between customers and suppliers, imposed by the American obsession with competition. This phenomenon has been particularly prevalent in government contracting.

3. Listening to the customer often means we have to hear negative feedback to which we would really rather not be exposed. Opening oneself up to criticism by the customer is difficult and requires personal courage.

(Continued on next page)

Table 4.1 Nine Reasons We Struggle with
a Committed Customer Focus

4. Effective techniques for discerning customers' needs, wants and expectations have not been developed or taught. We must develop better techniques to focus on customers' needs, and make sure our work force is trained and motivated to use these techniques.

5. Managers have made the assumption that all they need to do is tell their employees to treat customers well and it will happen. What happens more frequently, however, is employees treat customers the same way management treats employees. In many organizations, this translates to customers being treated like second class citizens, as this is the way employees have been treated by management.

6. It is easier for management to blame lack of clearly defined customer requirements on the customer, than it is to take responsibility and work hard to define customer needs/requirements.

7. Some organizations believe they have so many different customers with differing needs (that sometimes conflict) that to attempt to discern what "customers" need and satisfy their needs is difficult, if not impossible.

(Continued on next page)

Table 4.1 Nine Reasons We Struggle with
a Committed Customer Focus

8. Some organizations have difficulty recognizing "customers" and prefer believing they only have a "mission."

9. Individual or group performance is rarely appraised on customer satisfaction, especially internal customer satisfaction. This is especially true in organizations with "TURF-TYPE" systems.

Table 4.1 Nine Reasons We Struggle with
a Committed Customer Focus

Source: Total Quality: A Textbook of Strategic Quality, Leadership & Planning, Lam, Watson, and Schmidt, Air Academy Press, 1990.

Many texts have become so process focused that they have neglected the above issues. We must ensure that a well defined strategy exists for gaining knowledge in product/service development and design while also emphasizing process quality improvement.

Since 1980, process improvement has been one of the hottest topics in TQM literature, spreading across industry worldwide. Whether we are involved in the service or manufacturing industry we come face to face with some type of process each day. In a general sense, we will define a process as an activity that blends inputs in order to generate corresponding outputs. A general process diagram, also known as an Input-Process-Output (IPO) diagram, is displayed in Figure 4.3. Whether we are performing a service, producing a product, or completing a task, the choice of outputs to be measured should be based on how well the process performs with respect to customer (internal or external) requirements. Examples of specific output measures might be: 1) for a billing process we measure the time to complete a bill and the number of errors per bill; 2) for a machining process we measure the inner and outer diameters of a machined part; 3) for a composite material process we measure the material porosity and tensile strength; 4) for a mail sorting process we measure the time it takes to sort the mail and the proportion of misrouted mail; and 5) for a software installation/operational process we measure computation time and number of errors, among other key measures.

Specific IPO diagrams for the billing, machining, composite material, mail sorting and software processes (including key inputs) are shown in Figures 4.4, 4.5, 4.6, 4.7, and 4.8, respectively.

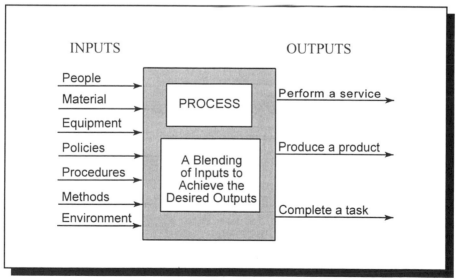

Figure 4.3 General Diagram of a Process

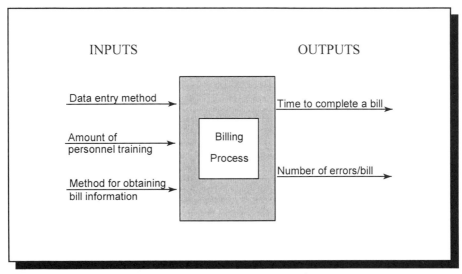

Figure 4.4 Billing Process Diagram

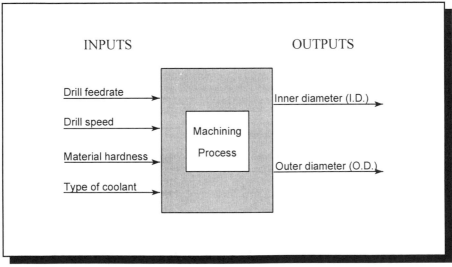

Figure 4.5 Machining Process Diagram

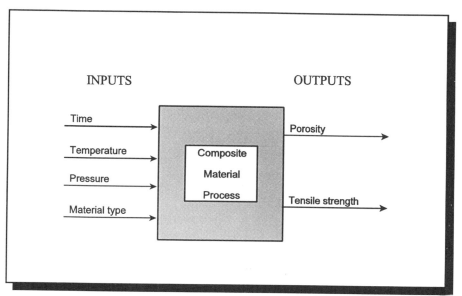

Figure 4.6 Composite Material Process Diagram

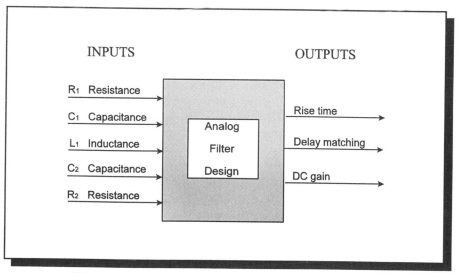

Figure 4.7 Analog Filter Design Process Diagram

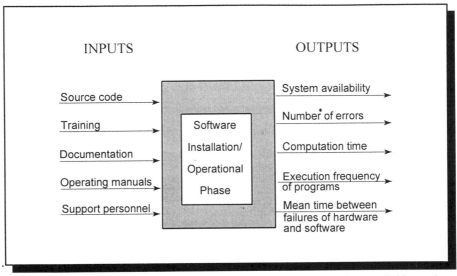

Figure 4.8 Installation/Operational Phase of the Software Lifecycle

To fully understand our processes and make continuous improvements necessitates the gathering, displaying and analysis of process data. The proper emphasis on measurement can probably not be put any more succinctly than the way Lord Kelvin expressed it over a century ago (1891):

"...When you can measure what you are speaking about and express it in numbers, you know something about it, but when you cannot express it in numbers, your knowledge is of a meagre and unsatisfactory kind."

Lord Kelvin

According to Peter Scholtes, author of *The Team Handbook* (Joiner Associates), there are generally six sources of problems associated with process knowledge:

1. **Lack of understanding of how a process actually works.**

2. **Lack of knowledge of how a process should work.**

3. **Errors and/or mistakes in executing process steps.**

4. **Practices which fail to recognize the need for preventive measures, such as maintenance or training.**

5. **Non-value added steps, activities which consume time and resources, but do not add value to the product or service.**

6. **Variation in inputs and outputs.**

Peter Scholtes

Obviously, effective process improvement methods must be able to identify and eliminate these six types of problems. Thus, the rest of this chapter will focus on strategies for doing just that.

SHEWHART AND DEMING CYCLES

An important aspect of the total quality philosophy is its emphasis on *continuous* improvement. This implies that an effective process improvement strategy be iterative in nature. Elimination of process problems must occur in a phased, continuous cycle. Dr. Walter A. Shewhart developed an approach to continuous improvement referred to as the **"PLAN - DO - CHECK - ACT"** OR **"PDCA"** cycle, which is illustrated in Figure 4.9 (Note: Deming used the term "STUDY" in place of "CHECK").

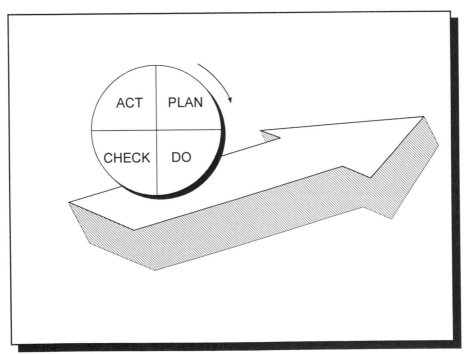

Figure 4.9 Shewhart Cycle

Simply stated, we first **plan** the improvement; then we **do** it; next we **check** some measurement to ensure it worked; and finally, we put it into **act**ion. Each phase of the cycle can be further described as indicated below:

PLAN – Identify and prioritize all possible processes. Then select the specific process to be improved. Map out the process using flow diagrams. Define the problem by clearly stating **what** it is, **where** and **when** it occurs, and **how** customer satisfaction can be measured using some process output. Analyze the process to identify possible causes of the process problem and focus on the most likely cause(s). Propose process improvement(s). Develop a data collection strategy.

DO – Develop Standard Operating Procedures (SOPs), and try out proposed improvement(s) on a small scale in a controlled environment. Monitor the improved process and document the result with data.

CHECK – Collect and analyze data to determine if the proposed improvements result in improved performance, lower cost, and reduced cycle time. Confirm results on a large scale. Use data to measure the amount of improvement.

ACT – Implement effective process changes by integrating them into the existing system of processes. Document all the improvement efforts.

Some companies that are just beginning a quality improvement program might find the PDCA cycle difficult to start. The planning phase is typically the problem because it is involved and not always intuitive in a problem-solving environment. A strategy referred to as FOCUS is often useful in breaking the "Planning" phase of the PDCA cycle into smaller components. Below is an outline of how FOCUS and PDCA can be used together.

Figure 4.10 Relationship Between FOCUS and PDCA

The Steps for FOCUS are as follows:

Step 1: Find a process to improve.

Where are the opportunities for improvement? They should be defined in terms of cost of poor quality (COPQ), not just in terms of failure rates; and this may necessitate the collection of data at this point. Sometimes it is best to gain confidence by attacking a simple problem and documenting the success. However, it will eventually be necessary to attack the hard problems. If a company is measuring its critical processes, knows where the variability is coming from, and can identify the costs associated with poor quality, then it will have little difficulty in prioritizing opportunities for improvement.

Step 2:   Organize a team that knows the process.

The team should include the process owner, customers (internal and external), people with knowledge of the process, and perhaps a facilitator. The team will need to establish meeting times, milestones, objectives and assign duties.

Step 3:   Clarify current knowledge of the process.

It is almost impossible to improve a process that is not well defined. Make sure everyone is using the same terminology, understands the objective, and knows how the process works. The time spent in building a good process flow diagram can often be the most beneficial in the improvement cycle.

Step 4:   Understand causes of process variation.

Causes of variability are the major culprits of high COPQ. Processes that have been documented with data can be observed before and after the process changes have been implemented. The tough part is identifying a cause for the variability. This may come from trial and error, from a brainstorming session, or from a designed experiment.

Step 5:   Select the process improvement.

Once we understand the problem, we need to select a solution. This involves weighing the cost of the improvement versus the benefit.

We highly recommend that you adapt the FOCUS/PDCA strategy to your own organization and develop your own "process" for improving processes (activities) and products/services. It should be one that all employees have bought into and that all levels of management espouse. A good example of such an adapted strategy is Apple Computer's "How To" Guide to AQM (Apple Quality Management) 7 Step Process shown in Table 4.2. Note the mapping of the process steps onto the PDCA cycle.

STEPS	ACTIONS	RESULT	TOOLS/ TECHNIQUES	PDCA CYCLE
1. State the Problem	Identify a process or problem to work on	An identified process Clearly defined quality goals	Brainstorming, Process Flow Diagram, Control Chart, Prioritization Matrices	P L A N
2. Describe Current Situation	Select a problem and a target for improvement	Data collected on a process over a period of time	Check Sheet, Pareto Diagram, Customer Interviews, Run Chart	
3. Identify Root Causes	Identify and Verify the root causes of the problem (5 whys)	Charts and Graphs to aid in analysis and decision making	Cause and Effect Diagram, Pareto Diagram, Scatter Diagram, Histogram, Check Sheet	
4. Take Corrective Action	Plan and Implement measurable actions that address the root causes	Action plan including timing of milestones Measures of progress	Process Flow Diagram, Force Field Analysis, Tree Diagram, Activity Network Diagram	D O
5. Measure Results	Confirm that the improvement target has been met	Comparison of before and after performance	Control Chart, Run Chart, Pareto Chart, Histogram, Customer Interviews	CHECK
6. Standardize the Process	Make sure everyone knows what the new process is	Update standardized process People trained and using the standard process	Process Flow Diagram, Procedures, Training, Control Chart	A C T
7. Recycle	Review the PDCA cycle to learn all that you can from the process	Knowledge to execute the PDCA process better next time	Brainstorming, Process Flow Diagram, Control Chart, Prioritization Matrices	PLAN

Table 4.2 "How To" Guide to AQM 7 Step Process

Source: Apple Computer, Inc., Fountain, CO

The strategies presented thus far are not new. They have been used by organizations around the world for many years. Sometimes they work and sometimes they don't. What makes one organization successful while another fails? As previously stated, one of the leading causes for failure is poor management support.

It is easy to say that management should support its employees if it is serious about process improvement. But management support must be more than providing money and time for training or giving a hearty "pat on the back" for a job well done. Conversely, employees need to be held accountable and provide a return on investment for their training. They are responsible for improving their processes, for their team efforts, and for their part in achieving the organizational mission, with or without management support.

> *"No man in the wrong can stand up against a man in the right who keeps on a-coming."*

Capt. Bill McDonald

Texas Rangers

The Six Sigma business initiative described in Appendix D attacks this support issue directly by establishing and nurturing an organizational infrastructure designed to guarantee ROI through both continuous and breakthrough improvement. The strategy for obtaining knowledge discussed next is the link between management support and a return on a training investment. See Figure 4.11.

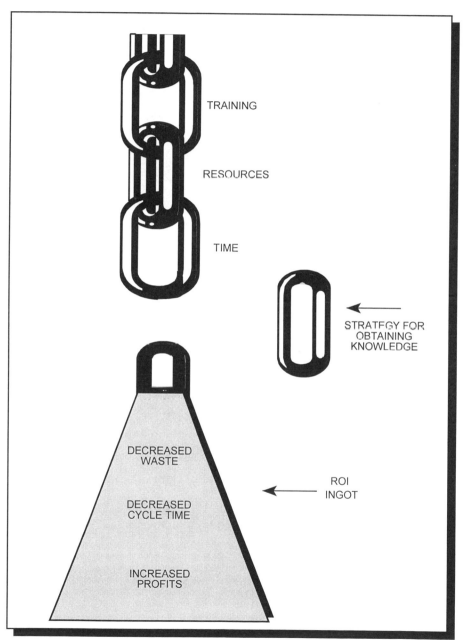

Figure 4.11 Missing Link for Obtaining ROI from
Quality Improvement

We now present in Table 4.3 a KBM strategy for gaining knowledge. The depth and breadth of our answers to these questions will determine our level of knowledge and, consequently, our ability to make good decisions. These questions are the heart and soul of the KBM-based Six Sigma Project Master Strategy discussed in Appendix D.

QUALITY IMPROVEMENT ORIENTED QUESTIONS MANAGERS NEED TO ASK THEIR PEOPLE!

1. What processes (activities) are you responsible for? Who is the owner of these processes? Who are the team members? How well does the team work together?

2. Which processes have the highest priority for improvement? How did you come to this conclusion? Where is the data that led to this conclusion?

For those processes to be improved,

3. How is the process performed?

4. What are your process performance measures? Why? How accurate and precise is your measurement system?

5. What are the customer driven specifications for all of your performance measures? How good or bad is the current performance? Show me the data. What are the improvement goals for the process?

(Continued on next page)

Table 4.3 Quality Improvement Oriented Questions
Managers Need To Ask Their People!

6. What are all the sources of variability in the process? Show me what they are.

7. Which sources of variability do you control? How do you control them and what is your method of documentation?

8. Are any of the sources of variability supplier-dependent? If so, what are they, who is the supplier, and what are we doing about it?

9. What are the key variables that affect the average and variation of the measures of performance? How do you know this? Show me the data.

10. What are the relationships between the measures of performance and the key variables? Do any key variables interact? How do you know for sure? Show me the data.

11. What setting for the key variables will optimize the measures of performance? How do you know this? Show me the data.

12. For the optimal settings of the key variables, what kind of variability exists in the performance measures? How do you know? Show me the data.

(Continued on next page)

Table 4.3 Quality Improvement Oriented Questions
Managers Need To Ask Their People!

13. How much improvement has the process shown in the past 6 months? How do you know this? Show me the data. 14. How much time and/or money have your efforts saved or generated for the company? How did you document all of your efforts? Show me the data.

Table 4.3 Quality Improvement Oriented Questions
Managers Need To Ask Their People!

These 14 questions can be partitioned into the following 4-step KBM process abbreviated as PCOR:

1. **P**rioritize (Questions 1-2)

2. **C**haracterize (Questions 3-10)

3. **O**ptimize (Questions 11-12)

4. **R**ealize (Questions 13-14)

Our claim is that if management asks its people the right questions, ensures its people are trained in the best practices to answer these questions, and if the organization provides a climate where people are motivated to improve quality, then return on investment will take place through better, faster, and lower cost products and services. The primary by-products of this approach will be reduced waste, increased profit margins, and "World Class" status. We will now examine each of these fourteen questions in detail.

> 1. **What processes (activities) are you responsible for? Who is the owner of these processes? Who are the team members? How well does the team work together?**

These seem like simple questions, and for most employees they should be easy to answer. However, we have seen several matrix-managed organizations where the answers to these questions are not always readily understood. Part of a manager's responsibility is to direct and support his/her people and that includes making sure they can answer these questions. If we ask the first question and find people struggling to answer it, chances are we have not communicated job responsibilities to our employees in a clear and concise manner.

For any team to function properly, it is also critical for everyone involved in a process to understand who all of the players are. Each team player must know what each person's responsibility is, to include who is ultimately responsible; that is: who's the process owner?

Team dynamics are also an important aspect of the knowledge gaining and quality improvement process. If a team does not consist of harmoniously working members who are in sync with a specific leader, there typically will be chaos. Also keep in mind that team members and/or team leaders who dominate to the point of shutting others off will hinder team performance. Likewise, team members who fail to participate or who pout after they don't get their way are not only non-functional, but can degrade team cohesiveness and performance. Managers need to know the value of each team member's contribution and have the ability to remove a person from the team if there is no value added.

> *"Real success comes with proper emphasis on goals and team problem solving."*

Kenneth O. Mooney

The success of the quality improvement process very much depends on the ability of management to foster teamwork and the team problem solving process. Consider the following excerpt from the article titled "Honesty Without Fear" by Theodore Lowe and Gerald McBean. The article appeared in the November 1989 issue of <u>Quality Progress</u>.

"A most compelling argument for changing the way managers think about their employees was provided in the following remarks made to a group of American businessmen by Konosuke Matsushita, executive director of Matsushita Electric Industrial Co.:

> 'We are going to win and the industrial west is going to lose out: there's nothing much you can do about it, because the reasons for your failure are within yourselves. Your firms are built on the Taylor Model; even worse, so are your heads. With your bosses doing the thinking while the workers wield the

screwdrivers, you're convinced deep down that this is the right way to run a business. For you, the essence of management is getting the ideas out of the heads of the bosses into the hands of labor.

We are beyond the Taylor Model; business, we know, is now so complex and difficult, the survival of firms so hazardous in an environment increasingly unpredictable, competitive, and fraught with danger, that their continued existence depends on the day-to-day mobilization of every ounce of intelligence. For us, the core of management is precisely the art of mobilizing and pulling together the intellectual resources of all employees in the service of the firm.'"

> *"Only by drawing on the combined brainpower of all its employees can a firm face up to the turbulence and constraints of today's environment."*

Konosuke Matsushita

In our experience the companies that successfully manage the team problem solving process are the ones that obtain the best ROI for their quality improvement effort. Motorola has over 3000 teams worldwide and has approximately doubled their sales revenue with the same number of employees in a four to five year period.

Another organization with great success in the team problem solving process is Freudenberg-NOK. In the May 15, 1995 issue of "Rubber and Plastics News" there *is an article titled "Day: Lean systems not for fainthearted." Joseph C. Day is the CEO of the company. In this article he points out that Freudenberg-NOK spends $750,000 annually on the improvement team process and gets a ten to twelve fold return on investment. The article also states that since 1989 "The company has... more than doubled its sales to $600 million using about 40 percent less [floor] space and the same number of employees working just five days a week rather than 6½ days..." Obviously, the team problem solving process can be very effective.*

The team problem solving process can be thought of as the engine that drives the quality improvement process. The successful teams in all areas within an organization will be using the tools to answer the questions that managers need ask. This is what makes Knowledge Based Management work.

You will notice that a few times in this text we reference job security as an outcome of the quality improvement process. This is a crucial result that management needs to plan for. It stands to reason that no one will work to improve productivity if that person expects to be laid off as a result. If a team improvement project improves productivity and eliminates the need of one person in an area, management needs to make a commitment to find that person another position. To lay that person off would be suicide to the improvement process.

Consider the following excerpt from a "Chicago Tribune" review of the book <u>The Loyalty Effect: The Hidden Force Behind Growth, Profits, and Lasting Value</u> *by Frederick F. Reichheld.*

1. Revenues and market share grow as the best customers are swept into the company's business, building repeat sales and referrals.

2. Sustainable growth enables the firm to attract and retain the best employees while consistently delivering superior value to customers. That in turn increases employees' loyalty by giving them pride and satisfaction in their work.

3. Loyal long-term employees learn on the job how to reduce costs and improve quality, which further enriches the customer-value proposition and generates superior productivity.

4. Upward-spiraling productivity coupled with increased efficiency of dealing with loyal customers generates the kind of cost advantage that is difficult for competitors to match.

From the above excerpt as well as the other cases cited and from numerous other examples, it is clear that companies successful in the improvement process can expect both increased revenues and market share. This makes it reasonable to commit to not reducing the work force as an outcome of an improvement project that results in increased efficiencies.

As you can see, the answers to this first set of questions that managers need to ask are crucial to the success of the entire process.

Tools and Techniques Used to Answer These Questions:
- *Communication*
- *Teamwork*
- *Common Sense*

> *"Teamwork is about getting 25 guys playing for the name on the front of their uniforms rather than the name on the back."*

Tommy Lasorda
Los Angeles Dodgers

> **2. Which processes have the highest priority for improvement? How did you come to this conclusion? Where is the data that led to this conclusion?**

Many people in industry are stressed out from working hard. Their plate (so to speak) is full and they are juggling many responsibilities. In this environment, the only way to keep from burning out and/or going insane is to have a clear understanding of the priorities. If employees don't understand their priorities, then it is management's responsibility to help them. Several things to consider in setting priorities are based on the scorecard philosophy discussed in Chapter 3. A list of further considerations should include the following:

Early Phases of Product/Service Development
1. *Marketing Strategies*
2. *Customer Needs*
3. *Cost of Delayed Market Entry*
4. *Cost of Possible Recall after Market Entry*
5. *Projected Sales*
6. *Profit Margin*
7. *Where in the Lifecycle the Activity is Located*

Later Phases of Product/Service Development

1. Yield
2. Cycle Times
3. Cost of Poor Quality
4. Customer Complaints
5. Profit Margin
6. Where in the Lifecycle the Activity is Located

When several different activities compete for limited resources, a comparison based on data collected on the above metrics will be helpful. This comparative analysis can help an individual and/or team identify the critical activities versus those less critical. Too often we have seen the selection of processes to be "reengineered" based on gut feel, rather than any kind of comparative analysis based on hard facts and data. Most organizations typically do not have the resources to attack every problem simultaneously. Hence, good decision-making at this point can and should lead to greater return on investment from the resources expended.

It is also important to note that many failed quality improvement efforts come as a result of trying to solve too big of a problem and/or trying to improve downstream activities when upstream ones are out of control.

Tools and Techniques Used to Answer These Questions:
- *Cost of Poor Quality Analysis*
- *Pareto Chart*
- *Teamwork*
- *Common Sense*

FOR THOSE PROCESSES TO BE IMPROVED

> ### 3. How is the process performed?

It is amazing how we can convince ourselves that this step is something everyone already understands. Especially when dealing with complex processes, it is not uncommon for each person on a team to have a different view of how an activity takes place. If all the players involved are not in agreement on how an activity is performed, there will inevitably be excess variation. Extraneous variation generates fires which in turn generate fire-fighting. Although fire-fighting may appear necessary in the short term, fire prevention is required to improve the bottom line in the long term.

The best approach to basic problem solving is to first map out every major step in an activity. Then carefully break down each major step into exactly how the process is performed. Although this question needs to be answered with words describing each step, the more we can use graphics the better the communication.

Failing to satisfactorily answer this question leads to aborted attempts at acquiring knowledge and unsuccessful transfers of an activity from:

      i)   *small scale to large scale*

     ii)   *site to site*

iii) one generation product/service to the next generation

iv) supplier to customer

Oftentimes a process flow diagram can reveal ways to reduce cycle time, defects, and non-value added activities.

Tools and Techniques Used to Answer This Question:
- *Process Flow Diagram*
- *Input-Process-Output (IPO) Diagram*
- *Teamwork*
- *Common Sense*

"If we can't agree on how to do something, how can we all do it right?"

Anonymous

---

4. **What are your process performance measures? Why? How accurate and precise is your measurement system?**

In order to improve any process there will have to be some measure(s) of performance, which are also referred to as process outputs. Since what we measure will drive the entire quality improvement process, it is paramount that we measure the right thing. Measures of performance should somehow represent a metric related to customer needs. If what we are measuring cannot be correlated to a customer (internal or external), it is probably a non-value added measurement. A good starting point for metric development is to answer the following questions:

1. *Who are my internal and external customers?*

2. *What are my customers' needs?*

3. *What measures of performance are related to those needs and which of these will give me feedback on how well the customer needs are being met?*

4. *How can I prioritize the measures of performance listed in (3) above?*

Many organizations, particularly those in the service sector, struggle with what it is that they should measure. Since almost every customer need is related in some way to cost, schedule (time), or performance, we suggest the following process—a matrix development approach—to generate potentially valid metrics. Here is how it works:

Step 1:   *Identify the critical processes that are essential for the success of the company.*

Step 2:   *Build a critical process/quality criteria matrix as shown in Table 4.4.*

Step 3:   *Fill in the definition portion of the matrix by defining each process in detail. Note that the process flow diagram is used for this purpose.*

Step 4:   *Brainstorm potential factors that affect the quality criteria. Performance, time, and cost criteria are shown in Table 4.4, but other criteria such as safety, ergonomics, and environment could also apply.*

Step 5:   *Select potential measures from the cause and effect diagram.*

Note that this process combines the use of some of the basic tools presented in Chapter 5: process flow, cause and effect diagram, and a matrix to synergize the effect of each of the tools individually.

Table 4.4 Critical Process / Quality Criteria Matrix

Another important part of this question is addressing our measurement system. We must carefully decide on how to measure our activity, the cost of the measurement system, and most importantly, the accuracy and precision of the measurement system. Gathering data on a process is a process in itself, and care should be taken to make this process as efficient as possible, while maintaining the accuracy and precision of the measurements themselves. Operational definitions (for example, definition of a defect) are of utmost importance and could have a significant impact on the measurement system.

Tools and Techniques Used to Answer These Questions:
- *QFD (to determine measures of performance related to customer needs)*
- *Gage Capability (to determine measurement system accuracy and precision)*
- *Teamwork*
- *Common Sense*

> **5. What are the customer driven specifications for all of your performance measures? How good or bad is the current performance? Show me the data. What are the improvement goals for the process?**

Using customer needs to derive the measures of performance (outputs) allows us to more easily determine optimal values and acceptable limits for our outputs. These acceptable limits are in reality our customer driven specifications. Ideally we should not arbitrarily set customer specifications. For example, consider a pilot production phase where we make some (3 to 30) prototypes and measure their individual parameters. Suppose one particular parameter, call it y, has its measured values stacked on a number line, as shown in Figure 4.12. We then compute the mean or average value (ȳ) and the standard deviation (σ or sigma) from the set of values. The spread from (ȳ - 3σ) to (ȳ + 3σ) represents the natural tolerances of the parameter y. If we set the specification limits for y at (ȳ - 3σ) and (ȳ + 3σ), these are in reality statistical limits that do not necessarily reflect customer needs.

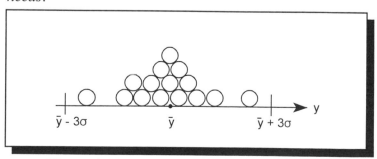

Figure 4.12 Measured Values of Parameter y

The customer should, in fact, be a part of the specification setting process. That means we need to dialogue with the customer. Keep in mind that some customers do not fully understand their needs or the capability of state-of-the-art technologies. Compromises may need to be made. Thus, the relationship between the supplier and customer should be one of open communications.

Another approach to setting targets and specifications is to benchmark the industry on similar products/services. This insures that the targets and specifications we selected will be competitive. However, it does not necessarily mean that our process is competitive. To determine how good or bad the current performance is requires us to look at how the voice of the process compares to the voice of the customer. In other words, we assess the process capability. To drive improvement of the capability measures, management and teams must work together to develop effective stretch goals and be held accountable for these goals.

Tools and Techniques Used to Answer These Questions:
- *QFD*
- *Benchmarking*
- *Control Charts*
- *Capability Study (C_{pk})*
- *Yield Analysis*
- *Teamwork*
- *Common Sense*

> **6. What are all the sources of variability in the process?
> Show me what they are.**

By now we should know all the outputs to be measured, their targets and specifications. The next obvious step is to identify every known variable that can possibly affect these outputs. The more complex the product/service or process (activity) the larger the number of sources of variability and the more crucial it is to answer this question. Some scientists and engineers use the complexity of their processes as an excuse for not trying to answer this question. Common sense should indicate that highly complex processes have so many variables in them that the brain cannot keep up with them day to day. Therefore, it is extremely important that they all be listed on a sheet of paper.

To ensure that all the variables are listed, it is best to form categories of sources of variation and to thoroughly think through each step in the process (activity). It is also important to list each source of variability in terms of a specific variable and not use general or abstract terms. For example, instead of listing the climate we should specify the following variables: temperature, humidity, pressure, altitude, wind speed, etc.

Theoretically, if we know all the sources of variability and tightly control each one, the outputs should be in control with low variability. Conversely, if we are not aware of some major sources of variability and/or they are left uncontrolled, we can expect the outputs to be out of control and/or vulnerable to excessive variability. Therefore, answering this question is necessary to control our processes and to reduce variability.

This is also a good place to brainstorm all possible failure modes, their effects and their causes. We should list every possible cause for failure in order to prioritize them and to prepare for finding a way to "foolproof" the process from these failures.

As a final note, the process of listing all the sources of variability and/or failure modes will not likely be complete the first time we do it. Therefore, this question needs to be re-visited, and any changes need to be documented and dated so that we will always know the current version used to answer this question.

Tools and Techniques Used to Answer This Question:
- *Cause and Effect (Fishbone or Ishikawa) Diagram*
- *Failure Mode and Effects Analysis (FMEA)*
- *Fault Tree Analysis (FTA)*
- *Teamwork*
- *Common Sense*

> **7. Which sources of variability do you control? How do you control them and what is your method of documentation?**

To successfully accomplish this task we need to consider every source of variability or failure in Question 6 and develop simple, low-cost Standard Operating Procedures (SOPs) for holding most of these variables constant and for foolproofing most of the causes of failure. These SOPs should be clearly stated and all employees trained and motivated to understand and comply with the SOPs. This is a critical step toward getting any process/activity into control and/or preventing product/service failures.

Many believe that the construction of and strict adherence to a set of SOPs for the purpose of controlling critical variables is a violation of the principles of Total Quality Management, which espouses liberal use of the ingenuity, creativity, and empowerment of people. Certainly ingenuity, creativity, and empowerment are desperately needed in the discovery of critical factors which affect our products/services and processes/activities. However, when these enviable human attributes are left to flounder in an unorganized and poorly managed scenario, the most likely result is chaos and fire-fighting, as depicted in Figure 4.13.

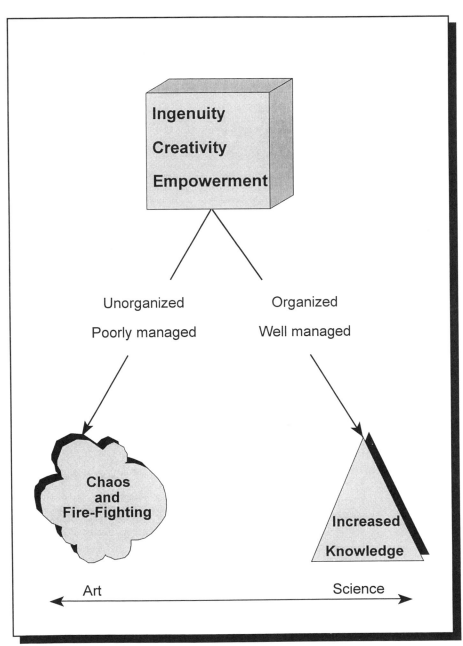

Figure 4.13 Capturing the Power of Ingenuity, Creativity,
and Empowerment

On the other hand, if ingenuity, creativity, and empowerment are properly harnessed in an organized and well managed scenario, we can make unbelievable advances in gaining knowledge. Knowledge Based Management is the key to transforming the art of management into a science.

Significant return on investment has been made in all types of products/services and processes through a concentrated effort in answering Questions 3-7. In particular, Questions 3, 4, 6, and 7 constitute a structured approach to basic problem solving and are the key essentials to practicing the scientific method.

The documentation for the most current answers to these questions should be placed in a notebook to serve as a library of product/service/process knowledge. The more precise and specific the answers are, the greater the level of knowledge. Any transfer of technology should also include the transfer of this notebook. Furthermore, the certification, registration, or qualification process under umbrellas such as ISO-9000, QS-9000, D1-9000, Quality Systems Review, Process Validation, Process Characterization, etc., will be greatly facilitated by simply repackaging the knowledge contained in this notebook.

Tools and Techniques Used to Answer These Questions:
- *Cause and Effect Diagram*
- *Teamwork*
- *Common Sense*

> **8.** **Are any of the sources of variability supplier-dependent?**
> **If so, what are they, who is the supplier, and what are**
> **we doing about it?**

If our suppliers are providing us with highly variable materials it may be difficult to magically develop product/services or processes without excessive variability in our outputs. It is best to find some key measures for our vendors' products and to produce histograms, run charts or control charts to evaluate the consistency of our incoming materials.

If we have evidence of excessive variation due to a specific supplier, it is advised that we help the supplier answer Questions 1 through 7 in order to improve the processes. This can be a very sensitive issue and each situation may have to be handled differently.

In general, there are six options for handling vendor variability problems:

i. *work with the vendors, helping them implement quality improvement;*

ii. *perform incoming inspection to selectively screen out non-conforming product;*

iii. *design an experiment to find a way to make the process robust (insensitive to vendor material variation);*

iv.   *find a better vendor;*

v.   *verify, validate, and possibly change the requirements;*

vi.   *redesign the product.*

Research and experience shows that option (i) is the most effective in gaining long-term ROI.

Tools and Techniques Used to Answer These Questions:
- *Histogram*
- *Run Chart*
- *Control Chart*
- *Design of Experiments (DOE)*
- *Brainstorming*
- *Teamwork*
- *Common Sense*

> **9.   What are the key variables that affect the average and variation of the measures of performance? How do you know this? Show me the data.**

In order to improve the measures of performance (outputs) for our process, knowledge of the variables which shift the average and/or standard deviation of the output is required.

The objective for almost any measure of performance will be to either:

1. *maximize the average value with low variation,*

2. *minimize the average value with low variation, or*

3. *achieve a target for the average value with low variation.*

To accomplish this task we need to know which inputs can be used to adjust the average output up or down and which inputs can be used to adjust the variation down.

When this information is not available from prior knowledge we will either need to analyze historical data or design an experiment. Certainly, prior knowledge, experience and a literature review can greatly reduce the number of inputs that will have to be investigated via experimentation.

Collecting and analyzing historical data or designing experiments for the purpose of making improvements requires that we first successfully answer Questions 1 through 8. If we fail to address these pre-data essentials it is likely that we will not gain "knowledge" and only fuel a raging fire of "chaos." Refer to Figure 4.13.

If we are in desperate need of finding inputs that lead to minimizing variation, it is worth noting that the most efficient and effective way to accomplish this task will be through a screening DOE described in Chapter 6.

Tools and Techniques Used to Answer These Questions:
- *Design of Experiments (DOE)*
- *Historical Data Modeling (Regression Analysis)*
- *Teamwork*
- *Common Sense*

> **10.** **What are the relationships between the measures of performance and the key variables? Do any key variables interact? How do you know for sure? Show me the data.**

Answering this question requires the use of historical data modeling or a modeling DOE. As stated in Question 9, either of these modeling approaches presupposes a heavy emphasis on Questions 1 through 8; otherwise, the models will not produce knowledge.

Every process has a true physical model. However, when the theory is not available to produce the true physical model, we need to go to the process itself and ask it questions. Design of Experiments (DOE) is the discipline of interrogating a process in a systematic and efficient manner for the purpose of discovering how the input factors affect the output. A properly designed experiment will produce an accurate model which should closely approximate the true physical model. Knowledge of a process at this level of detail translates into competitive advantage. Characterization, optimization, sensitivity, tolerance setting, and trade-off analyses are now possible.

Tools and Techniques Used to Answer These Questions:
- *Design of Experiments (DOE)*
- *Historical Data Modeling (Regression Analysis)*
- *Teamwork*
- *Common Sense*

> **11. What setting for the key variables will optimize the measures of performance? How do you know this? Show me the data.**

Knowing the model for the average response and the model for the standard deviation of the response allows us to determine the settings for the key variables which will optimize our objectives. By having the models, we have the necessary knowledge to optimize. Furthermore, if costs about the input variables are known, the models can be used to accomplish cost/benefit trade-off analyses. Without the models, our knowledge of our products, services and/or associated processes is limited. Thus, we also limit our ability to make the best decisions to achieve better, faster, and lower cost results.

Tools and Techniques Used to Answer These Questions:
- *Design of Experiments (DOE)*
- *Historical Data Modeling (Regression Analysis)*
- *Teamwork*
- *Common Sense*

> **12. For the optimal settings of the key variables, what kind of variability exists in the performance measures? How do you know? Show me the data.**

Once optimal input variable settings are determined, practitioners should always validate the model through what experimenters call confirmatory runs. Confirmatory runs not only tell us if the model predicts well, but also tell us what kind of variability exists in the output (or performance measure). Before we even do confirmatory runs, the models allow us to predict what our average response should be and what the standard deviation should be when we run the process under the optimal input variable settings. If the confirmatory runs fall within the predicted interval, we say we have confirmed the model. If enough confirmation runs are performed, we can estimate the process capability.

Tools and Techniques Used to Answer These Questions:

- *Design of Experiments (DOE)*
- *Statistical Process Control (SPC)*
- *Capability Study (C_{pk})*
- *Teamwork*
- *Common Sense*

13. How much improvement has the process shown in the past 6 months? How do you know this? Show me the data.

The answers to Questions 13 and 14 require the use of a scorecard to record process improvement over time. Examples of computable measures of quality include defects per unit (dpu), C_{pk}, cycle time, or COPQ. We would be hard pressed to convince anyone that our process has improved if our scorecard for COPQ appeared as shown in Figure 4.14.

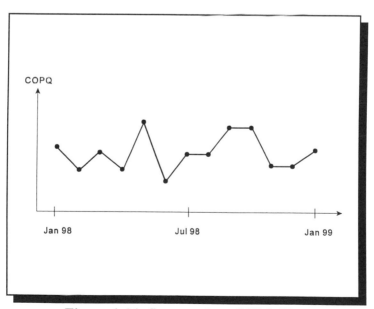

Figure 4.14 Scorecard on COPQ That
Does Not Depict Process Improvement

On the other hand, a scorecard that looks like the one in Figure 4.15 may indeed be indicative of improvement.

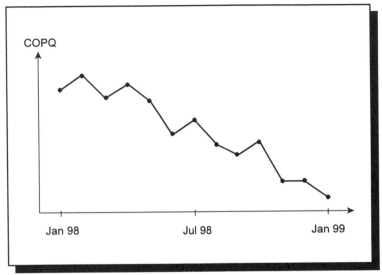

Figure 4.15 Scorecard on COPQ That
Does Depict Process Improvement

*We say "may be indicative" because if this is true process improvement, we will know **why** COPQ is going down. That is, if we were to do it all over again, it would be repeatable and we would have the documentation that links what we did with the results.*

Tools and Techniques Used to Answer These Questions:
- *Run Chart*
- *Control Chart*
- *COPQ Analysis*
- *Teamwork*
- *Common Sense*

> **14. How much time and/or money have your efforts saved or generated for the company? How did you document all of your efforts? Show me the data.**

The results depicted in Figure 4.15 must be correlated with the company's bottom line. That is, we don't want optimization of one process to cause deterioration in other areas or processes of the company. Localized versus global optimization can be a problem, especially in companies where keeping score is synonymous with gathering evidence to fire someone. Management must ensure that scorecards are implemented in a way that motivates people to play to win but to do so in an ethical manner without feeling the pressure to falsify data. Advanced charting techniques can sometimes detect the presence of falsified data, but the key is to prevent this from happening in the first place. Solid knowledge about people, processes, products, and organizations is the key to an honest, ethical, and winning scorecard that generates real return on investment and enhances job security.

Tools and Techniques Used to Answer These Questions:
- *Run Chart*
- *Control Chart*
- *Correlation Studies*
- *Teamwork*
- *Common Sense*

This concludes our discussion of each of the 14 questions which management needs to ask. These questions represent the implementation strategy for a Knowledge Based Management system and provide managers with something they can actually do to promote quality improvement. Managers who ask these questions are on track to become leaders in developing their people and improving their processes. The answers to these questions provide the knowledge which drives the actual process improvement.

Hopefully, the reader has noticed the tools and techniques that were listed for each question. Appendix B provides the reader with a quick reference guide to the questions and the tools needed to answer each question. Appendix D shows how these 14 questions are partitioned into the four phases of the Six Sigma Project Master Strategy. The next two chapters address in more detail the tools and techniques needed to answer these questions.

Chapter 5

BASIC TOOLS AND TECHNIQUES TO OBTAIN KNOWLEDGE

"Ignorance is the curse of God,
Knowledge the wing wherewith we fly to heaven."

Shakespeare

By now you should know that Knowledge Based Management is both a management philosophy and strategy which, if properly implemented, will lead to improved decision-making throughout the entire organization. Successful implementation hinges on the proper, proactive involvement of management at all levels. Quality managers, middle managers, directors, vice-presidents, . . . *all* must be able to ask the right questions of their employees.

This chapter presents some basic tools to help employees answer these questions. It is management's responsibility to provide the tools and training so that employees have the opportunity to answer the questions effectively. The tools presented here are some of the most basic and most commonly used tools. Certainly, many other tools are available, but we provide these as an introduction to a few of the techniques that have proven to provide immediate results with essentially minimal investment.

Many of these tools are taken from *Basic Statistics: Tools for Continuous Improvement*. The reader is referred to this source for a more detailed explanation of the tools presented here as well as a more comprehensive list of tools.

AFFINITY DIAGRAM

An affinity diagram is a technique for organizing verbal information into a visual pattern. It starts with specific ideas and helps us work toward broad categories. Completing an affinity diagram is usually a group technique that is initiated by writing the problem or issue on a blackboard or flipchart for the group to see. Using brainstorming, we try to identify all facets of the problem and record them on sticky notes or index cards. We then cluster the specific ideas or sticky notes into major categories. We do this by asking "What ideas are similar?" and "Is this idea related to any of the others?" For each group, create a separate affinity card that describes the group. The resulting affinity diagram is a hierarchical structure that will give you valuable insight into the problem.

As an example, consider a situation where a group brainstormed what they believed to be "Barriers to Quality Improvement" in their organization. The ideas were recorded and grouped into various categories. The resulting affinity diagram in Table 5.1 shows the various perceived barriers.

Management

- Unclear direction
- Not willing or knowledgeable to ask the right questions
- Too many layers
- Wants immediate results versus substantial growth in knowledge through use of scientific method
- Don't track the right metrics
- Continued emphasis on old ways of doing business
- Reluctant to support new methods

Time

- Too busy fire-fighting
- Improper time management
- Duplicated effort
- Too many arguments without facts and data
- Too many unproductive meetings
- Too busy reorganizing

Communications

- Poor documentation
- Culture not right for sharing information
- Poor knowledge of customer needs
- Communicate to managers with emotion instead of facts, data and dollars
- Tools for properly communicating process information not known or used

Training

- Not enough people properly trained
- Inability to think and use common sense
- Management last to be trained versus first
- Need for follow-up assistance
- Suppliers need to be trained
- Unqualified trainers

Resources

- Limited resources
- Insufficient manpower
- Insufficient internal experts to assist others
- Improper allocation of resources

Reward System

- Promotes fire-fighting
- People not held accountable
- People (groups) compete against each other versus helping

Attitude and Motivation

- Critical and/or negative attitudes
- Resistance to change
- Fear of failure using new methods
- Unwilling to share what you know with others

Table 5.1 Affinity Diagram Example for
Barriers to Quality Improvement

BENCHMARKING

Benchmarking involves gathering information on "best" practices from the following:

1. Other divisions within the organization,
2. Competitors, and
3. Organizations that perform functionally equivalent activities.

The typical steps of a benchmarking exercise include:

1. Form a team to represent the area of concern.
2. Select the specific activity to be benchmarked.
3. Identify measures of performance for the activity.
4. Identify benchmark organizations.
5. Collect the data.
6. Perform a comparative analysis and identify the gaps.
7. Discuss the findings and set priorities for gap closure.
8. Implement and improve plans.
9. Start over.

The results of a benchmarking effort should provide us with knowledge of the following:

1. Who the industry leaders are,
2. How we are doing compared to industry leaders, and
3. What our priorities are for process improvement.

CAUSE AND EFFECT DIAGRAM

Also called an Ishikawa diagram or fishbone diagram, the cause and effect diagram is one of the most widely used quality improvement tools. It graphically depicts the relationship between a given response and the factors that influence this response. It is a structured approach to brainstorming potential causes for a given effect. It can be used as a dynamic documentation tool and can be very useful in variance reduction.

We begin building the cause and effect diagram by placing the response variable, problem, goal or objective at the "head" of the fish (see Figure 5.1). We then label the major categories that influence the effect being studied (for example, policies, human resources, machine, method, environment). These major categories will help trigger ideas in the brainstorming session and provide a balanced approach to brainstorming. The goal of the brainstorming session is to identify all the possible variables that can affect the response.

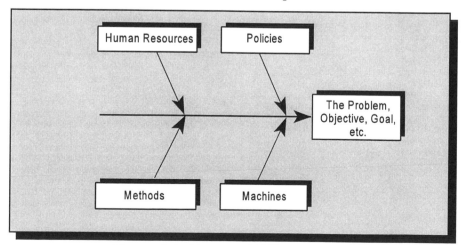

Figure 5.1 Cause and Effect Diagram

Finally, we classify or label each variable with a "C", "N", or "X" as follows:

C (constant).   These are variables that we have decided to hold constant in order to achieve the desired response or perhaps to reduce extraneous variation in the response. For each "constant" variable, a Standard Operating Procedure (SOP) should exist to tell us how the variable is being controlled.

N (noise).   These are the uncontrolled or noise variables. Although they may affect the response, they may be too expensive or too difficult to hold constant.

X (experimental). If an experiment is to be run (see Design of Experiments in Chapter 6), these are the variables (or factors) to be investigated. Not all cause and effect diagrams will have "X" factors. However, a variable that is a "C" today could become an "X" tomorrow if we should decide to investigate that variable's effect experimentally (and vice versa).

   The following example illustrates a cause and effect diagram for a gas mileage problem. The variables identified in Figure 5.2 are those identified to affect gas mileage. In Table 5.2, we classify the variables and decide to experiment with various gas types, oil types, and fuel additives.

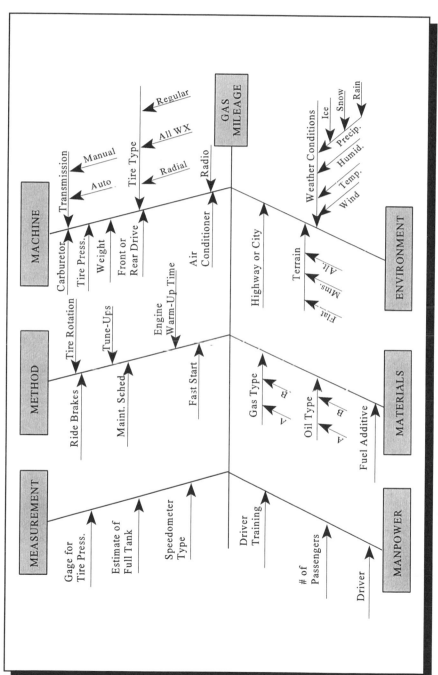

Figure 5.2 Cause and Effect Diagram for Gas Mileage

CONSTANTS	NOISE	EXPERIMENTAL
- Fast Start	- Engine Warm-Up	- Gas Type
- Ride Brakes	Time	- Oil Type
- Tire Rotation	- Carburetor	- Fuel Additive
- Tune-Ups	- Air Conditioning	
- Maintenance	- Driver	
Schedule	- # of Passengers	
- Transmission	- Highway vs City	
- Gage for Tire	- Weather Conditions	
Pressure	- Terrain	
- Estimate of Full	- Radio	
Tank	- Weight	
- Speedometer		
Type		
- Driver Training		
- Front Wheel		
Drive		
- Tire Type		

Table 5.2 CNX Identification for Gas Mileage Example

COMMON SENSE

In Chapter 4 we listed common sense as one of the tools that is needed to answer the Questions Managers Need to Ask. Many employers and bosses will talk about the need for common sense in their workforce but find it difficult to define. Most dictionaries will use the synonym "good judgment," while academicians may refer to it as "critical thinking." In either case, the definition is still vague.

However, if we look at R. Ennis' 13 dispositions of a critical thinker (*Critical Thinking and Subject Specificity*), we actually see the traits that someone with common sense should demonstrate. See Table 5.3.

• **Be open minded**
• **Take a position (and change a position) when evidence and reasons are sufficient to do so**
• **Consider the total situation**
• **Try to be well informed**
• **Seek as much precision as the subject permits**
• **Deal in an orderly manner with the parts of a complex whole**
• **Look for alternatives**
• **Seek reasons**
• **Seek a clear statement of the issue**
• **Keep in mind the original or basic concern**
• **Use and mention credible sources**
• **Remain relevant to the point**
• **Be sensitive to others' feelings, level of knowledge, and degree of sophistication**

Table 5.3 Thirteen Dispositions of the Critical Thinker

Source: R. Ennis: *Critical Thinking and Subject Specificity*

While it is nearly impossible to define common sense, we seem to know it when we see it. This table provides a list of the traits we expect to see in someone who is using common sense.

FAILURE MODE AND EFFECTS ANALYSIS (FMEA)

Failure Mode and Effects Analysis (FMEA) is a procedure used to identify and assess risks associated with potential product or process failure modes. By identifying risk, resources can be allocated to eliminate or reduce catastrophic failures. FMEA is generally accomplished early in the design phase of a new product or process or when design changes occur.

In Table 5.4 we see a simplified example of FMEA applied to an automobile design. Here, we have identified several components with associated possible failures. The "P" column is then used to assign a number that represents the probability of occurrence—the likelihood that we might see this failure in production. This number is subjectively assigned, based on our best judgment, since we may not have actually produced the item yet. Next, we assign numbers (S) that represent the seriousness of failure. For example, a brake failure would be more serious than an air conditioner failure. The risk (R) is the product of P times S $(R = P*S)$. Component failures can then be ranked from highest to lowest using this number. In our example, brake failure and engine overheat failure tie as the most serious failures. The next step in FMEA is to brainstorm possible causes of these failures and develop a plan to "foolproof" or eliminate them.

Product: Automobile

Component	Possible Failure	P	Effect of Failure on Product/User	S	R	Potential Cause(s)	How can Failure Be Eliminated/Reduced?
Windshield Washer	Failure to squirt washer fluid on windows	4	Safety hazard under certain environmental conditions	1	4	No fluid in reservoir; Supply line disconnected	Check fluid levels regularly
Battery	Does not retain charge	2	Dimmed lights; Car won't start	4	8	Loose connection; Dry/dead battery	Service the battery regularly or buy service-free battery
Brakes	Brakes fail	1	Can't stop car	10	10	Worn brake pads; No brake fluid	Check fluids, and replace worn pads
Engine	Overheats	2	Engine damage	5	10	Radiator hose worn/disconnected	Replace worn radiator hoses and check for good connections
Engine	Sputters and/or dies	1	Car stops and cannot be driven	8	8	Out of gas; Clogged jet; Fuel pump failure	Heed warning lights; good maintenance habits
Air Conditioner	Blows only warm air	3	Decreased comfort under certain environmental conditions	1	3	No freon; Compressor problem	Replace/add freon and check A/C regularly

P = probability of occurrence: 1 = extremely low ... 5 = moderate ... 10 = extremely high
S = seriousness of failure: 1 = very low .... 5 = significant ... 10 = catastrophic
R = P∗S = risk estimate: 1 = negligible risk ... 100 = extremely critical risk

Table 5.4 FMEA Example

FAULT TREE ANALYSIS

Fault Tree Analysis (FTA) is a deductive analytical technique used to move from the "Possible Failure" column in Table 5.4 to the column labeled "Potential Causes." It is a visual tool that provides an efficient and convenient format for conducting either qualitative or quantitative systems analysis. For example, it could be used to determine the probability of occurrence for one of the possible failures. Figure 5.3 shows a very simplistic FTA for "Engine Sputters and/or Dies," the fifth row in Table 5.4. For more information on FMEA and FTA, reference D.H. Stamatis (*Failure Mode & Effect Analysis*).

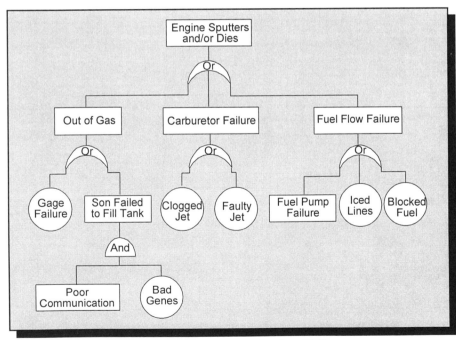

Figure 5.3 FTA for Engine Failure

HISTOGRAM

A histogram is a bar chart for numerical variables. It gives a pictorial representation of how the data are distributed. It is useful for visualizing the central tendency and variability of a data set.

In Table 5.5, we have an example data set. These numbers represent average gas mileage for a motor pool over a given period of time. In developing our histogram, we first need to decide how many classes we will use in summarizing the data. For 50 data points, we would generally use 5 to 7 classes (reference *Basic Statistics: Tools for Continuous Improvement*). Let's say that for this example we decide to use 6 classes. Next, we build a set of classes that will contain all of our data. Since our smallest data point is 8 and our largest is 45, we need classes that will cover this range. If we label our classes as shown in Table 5.6, we can place each data point in an individual class.

18	16	30	29	28	21	17	41	8	17
32	26	16	24	27	17	17	33	19	18
31	27	23	38	33	14	13	26	11	28
21	19	25	22	17	12	21	21	25	26
23	20	22	19	21	14	45	15	24	34

Table 5.5 Gas Mileage Data

Class	Values
6 to less than 12	8, 11
12 to less than 18	16, 16, 17, 17, 14, 12, 14, 17, 17, 13, 15, 17
18 to less than 24	18, 21, 23, 19, 20, 23, 22, 22, 19, 21, 21, 21, 21, 19, 18
24 to less than 30	26, 27, 25, 29, 24, 28, 27, 26, 25, 24, 28, 26
30 to less than 36	32, 31, 30, 33, 33, 34
36 to less than 42	38, 41
42 to less than 48	45

Table 5.6 Classes for Gas Mileage Data

Finally, we place this data in a bar graph as shown in Figure 5.4. The histogram gives us a much better picture of what our gas mileage looks like. We see that most of the values are between 12 and 30 mpg with 18-24 mpg representing the center. The data are somewhat skewed to the right by a few high mileage values.

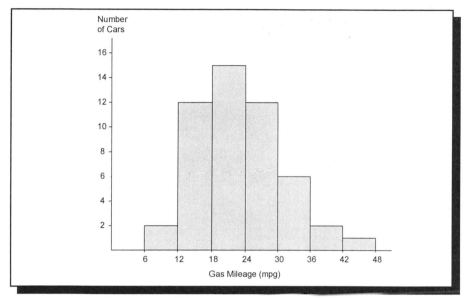

Figure 5.4 Histogram of Gas Mileage Data

INPUT-PROCESS-OUTPUT (IPO) DIAGRAM

The IPO diagram is a visual representation of a process or activity. It lists input variables and output characteristics. It is useful in defining a process and recognizing the relationships between input variables and responses.

In building an IPO diagram, we first choose a process. Next, we define the output(s). They are sometimes called the "quality characteristics" of the process. They are usually defined from a customer perspective. That is, we ask "What characteristics make this process valuable to the customer?" or "What key responses define this process as good or bad from a customer perspective?" We then need to define the input factors. This is best done using a cause and effect diagram. Usually, a process will have many more inputs than outputs.

As an example, consider the plastic molding process shown in Figure 5.5. The three outputs listed are not the only outputs but they are the ones that have been identified as important to the customer. The inputs were developed from a cause and effect diagram and should be classified by CNX (see Cause and Effect section).

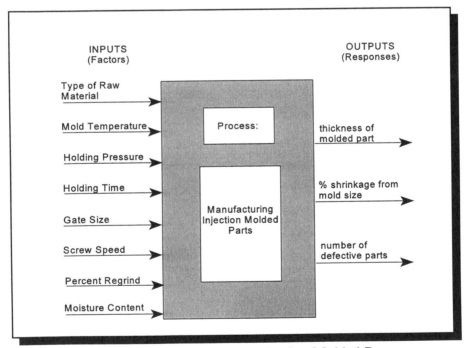

Figure 5.5 Manufacturing Injection Molded Parts

MEASURES OF CENTRAL TENDENCY

The two most common measures of central tendency are the mean and the median.

The **mean** is the arithmetic average, denoted by x̄. We obtain this value by adding all the numbers in the data set and dividing by the number of values in the data set. For example, if we look at the following data set,

Data Set: 8, 3, 7, 4, 5, 6, 30, 4, 4, 6,

the mean is given by:

$$\bar{x} = \frac{8 + 3 + 7 + 4 + 5 + 6 + 30 + 4 + 4 + 6}{10} = \frac{77}{10} = 7.7$$

The **median** is the middle value and is denoted by x̃.   To calculate the median, we need to order the data from smallest to largest and find the middle value. If we order the data set above, we get:

Ordered data: 3, 4, 4, 4, 5, 6, 6, 7, 8, 30

↑

middle value

Since there are an even number of values, we take the average of the two middle values, 5 and 6, so x̃ = 5.5. Here we see that the median is more representative of the center of the data than the mean. This is because the mean is more sensitive than the median to outlying values.

When data are highly skewed and/or contain outliers, we often use the median as a measure of central tendency.

The subject of outliers is worth dealing with in light of the fact that so many industries are plagued with this problem. As previously shown, outliers can distort our analysis. Thus, the most important strategy for dealing with outliers is to prevent them. The cause of outliers is one or more of the following:

1. Inadequate Standard Operating Procedures (SOPs),
2. SOPs not followed, or
3. Noise (uncontrolled) variables.

Certainly a team should address an outlier problem as early as possible. The key to successfully identifying specific causes of outliers and then removing these causes will be a thorough effort on the following:

1. Process flow diagram,
2. Cause and effect diagram with CNX and SOPs, and
3. FMEA.

If we have not prevented the occurrence of outliers and they appear in our data, then we need to consider the following:

1. Do not remove an outlying value from product test data or a capability analysis unless we have identified the assignable cause and removed it.

2. Perform statistical analyses with and without the outlier(s) and if the conclusions are radically different, try to confirm them both to discern the true relationship.

MEASURES OF DISPERSION

The three common measures of dispersion are the range, the variance, and the standard deviation.

The *range* is the number obtained by subtracting the smallest value from the largest value. Using the following data set,

Data Set X: 8, 3, 7, 4, 5, 6, 30, 4, 4, 6,

Range = 30 - 3 = 27.

The *sample variance*, denoted by S^2, is "almost" an average squared distance to the mean. In calculating the variance, we subtract the mean from each data point, square this value, add and then divide by one less than the number of values given. In our data set, the variance is:

$$S^2 = \frac{(8 - 7.7)^2 + (3 - 7.7)^2 + (7 - 7.7)^2 + ... + (6 - 7.7)^2}{9} = \frac{574.1}{9} = 63.79$$

The *sample standard deviation*, denoted by S, is simply the square root of the variance. The advantage of working with the standard deviation is that it has the same units as the mean and the individual data values. If we are measuring in centimeters, then the standard deviation is also given in centimeters. In our example, the standard deviation is:

$$S = \sqrt{63.79} = 7.99$$

NOMINAL GROUP TECHNIQUE

Nominal Group Technique is a structured method used to generate and rank order a list of ideas. To initiate a session using this technique, we assemble the group and define the problem or response that we wish to investigate. Each member then silently writes down as many ideas as possible. These ideas are then collected and recorded on a board or flipchart. For example, a team of five was assembled to identify problems in an office. Several complaints had been made but they were vague and gave the office manager little to work with. Table 5.7 shows the results of this team's list of problems.

The following office problems were identified in a silent brainstorming session:

    A. Ineffective organizational structure.
    B. Poor communications outside the office.
    C. Lack of training.
    D. Poor communications within the office.
    E. Unclear mission and objectives.
    F. Poor distribution of office mail.
    G. Lack of feedback on reports to management.
    H. Inadequate workspace.
    I. Lack of leadership.
    J. Poor computer support.

Table 5.7 Nominal Group Technique Example

The next step is to prioritize this list of items. One way to do this is to let each team member rank order each item on the list and then sum the scores for each item to generate a combined, prioritized list. Each of the five team members ranks the 10 items, with the highest ranking being a 10 and the lowest ranking a 1. The results of these rankings might appear as follows:

Problem	Person					Total	Priority
	1	2	3	4	5		
A	8	4	7	10	5	34	
B	7	9	8	8	10	42	High
C	1	1	2	3	3	10	
D	9	6	6	9	4	34	
E	10	8	9	7	9	43	High
F	6	10	5	6	1	28	
G	5	7	4	5	7	28	
H	2	2	1	1	2	8	
I	4	5	10	2	8	29	
J	3	3	3	4	6	19	

A Pareto chart on the "Total" column could now be accomplished to show what the high priority problems are.

PARETO CHART

A Pareto chart is a bar chart for non-numerical categories that rank orders the bars from highest to lowest and is used to identify the "heavy hitters." It is based on the "Pareto Principle" which says that 80% of the effects are due to 20% of the causes. In the following example, we have two Pareto charts showing the causes of problems with integrated circuit boards. The Pareto chart in Figure 5.6 shows that soldering is a major factor when we look at the total number of defects.

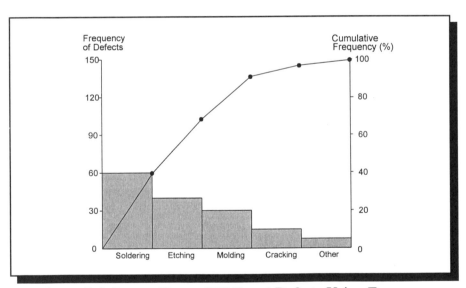

Figure 5.6 Pareto Chart of IC Board Defects Using Frequency

However, if we change the metric and look at monetary loss, Figure 5.7 shows that etching problems are really costing us far more than soldering problems.

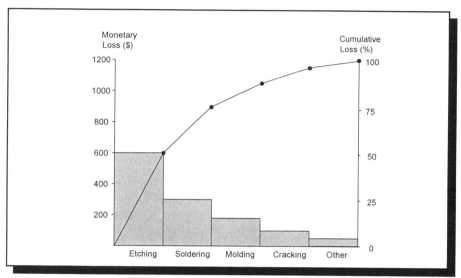

Figure 5.7   Pareto Chart of IC Board Defects
Using Monetary Loss

The cumulative line graph shown on these Pareto charts is read from the right vertical axis.   For example, Figure 5.7 shows that approximately 75% of the total monetary loss can be attributed to the first two categories, namely Etching and Soldering.

"*Data without concepts is blind.*
Concepts without data are empty."

Immanuel Kant

PROCESS CAPABILITY MEASUREMENTS

In this section we look at three metrics that are commonly used to describe the capability of a process. Most are calculated under the assumption that the critical measurements are normally distributed.

Figure 5.8 shows a distribution of critical measurements for a certain product with upper and lower specification limits (USL and LSL). All products with the critical measurement between the specification limits are classified as acceptable; the products with critical measurements outside the specification limits (shaded areas) are classified as defects. The metrics we will look at, dpm, C_p, and C_{pk}, all give a numerical value that indicates how well the process is doing with respect to these specification limits.

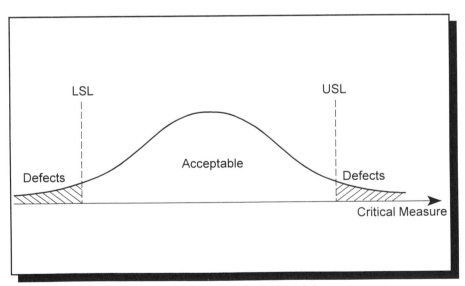

Figure 5.8 Distribution of Critical Measurements

The first measurement is *dpm*—defects per million. In the previous figure, dpm is represented by the proportion of area outside specification limits multiplied by one million. For example, if 3.5% of the area (equivalent to a proportion of .035) is outside specification limits, then we would expect 35,000 dpm. See Figure 5.9.

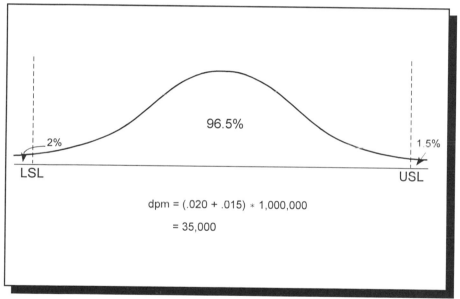

Figure 5.9 Defects per Million—dpm

A commonly used measure of process potential is C_p which is defined as:

$$C_p = \frac{USL - LSL}{6\sigma},$$

where σ is the standard deviation of the process.

When a process mean is not on Target (reference Figure 5.10), C_{pk} is used to measure the actual process capability. C_{pk} is defined as:

$$C_{pk} = \frac{(\# \text{ of std. dev's. between the process mean and the nearest spec limit})}{3}$$

In Figure 5.10, $\quad C_{pk} = \frac{3}{3} = 1.0, \quad$ and $\quad C_p = \frac{108 - 92}{6*2} = \frac{16}{12} = 1.33.$

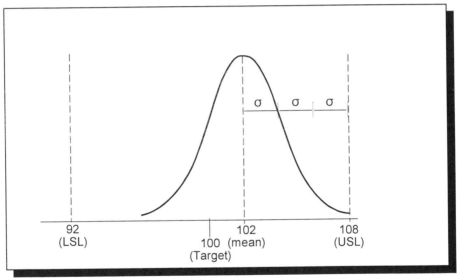

Figure 5.10 $\quad C_{pk} = 1.0 \quad$ and $\quad C_p = 1.33$

C_{pk} values below 1.0 are generally representative of poor processes. Conversely, C_{pk} values above 1.5 are generally representative of very competitive processes. The formal statistical definition of the term 6σ (Six Sigma) is $C_p = 2.0$, $C_{pk} = 1.5$, and dpm = 3.4. However, Six Sigma is much more than statistics. It is a business strategy for delivering ***better, faster, and lower cost products and services***. See Appendix D for more detail.

PROCESS FLOW DIAGRAM

A process flow diagram (sometimes called a flowchart) is a visual representation of all the major steps in a process. It helps us understand the process better, identify critical or problem areas, and identify improvements.

In building a process flow diagram, we will use four standard symbols. They are shown in Table 5.8.

This Symbol...	*Represents...*	*Some Examples are...*
(rounded rectangle)	Start/Stop	Receive Trouble Report Machine Operable
(diamond)	Decision Point	Approve/Disapprove Accept/Reject Yes/No Pass/Fail
(rectangle)	Activity	Drop Off Travel Voucher Open Access Panel
(circle)	Connector (to another page or part of the diagram)	(diagram with decision and activity connected to A and B)

Table 5.8 Process Flow Diagram Symbols

There are a few things to remember when charting a process:

1.   For a big process start by charting only the major steps or activities. Later on, chart these major activities separately in more detail.

2.   Remember that some processes may be "dynamic." (This is a fancy word we use when not everyone can agree on how the process runs.) When the process is difficult to define, it may be necessary to build a process flow diagram depicting how the process *should* run.

3.   If you find yourself getting wrapped up in details of the process, combine these details into a single larger activity and use one box. Come back to this box later if necessary.

The simple example, in Figure 5.11, shows the appointment process in a hospital. This diagram might be the first step in drawing up a more detailed process flow diagram. For instance, when the patient describes the type of care required, the operator may have many questions that are asked in order to help the patient. This block may be shown as a separate process flow diagram.

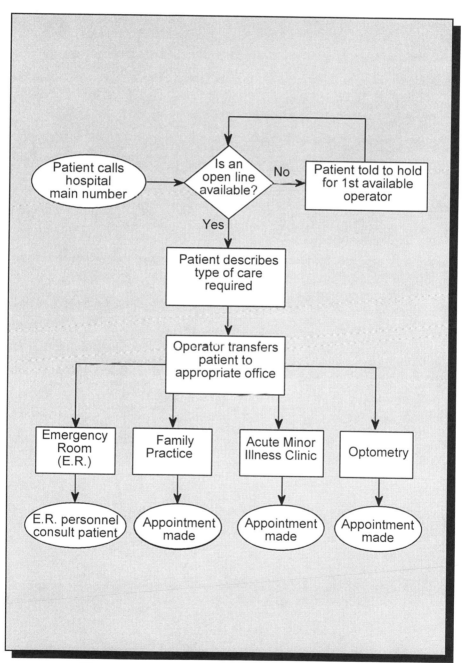

Figure 5.11 Hospital Appointment Process Flow

QUALITY FUNCTION DEPLOYMENT (QFD)

QFD is a systematic process used to integrate customer requirements into every aspect of the design and delivery of products and services. It is a tool that leads to focused technology development in spite of conflicting system requirements and seemingly divergent customer needs. The use of QFD provides a structure for identifying those design characteristics that contribute most (and least) to customer requirements.

The basic elements of QFD are not difficult to understand. However, the application of QFD can be a tedious and exhaustive process. QFD uses a series of matrices and charts that guide the project team through the activities of identifying customer needs and technical design requirements for each phase of product development. This produces direct linkage from customer requirements through product specifications, process design, and procedures (SOPs). When used correctly, QFD can help create products and processes with reduced costs, improved quality, features that satisfy customers and significantly shorter development times. For more information on QFD see *Basic Statistics: Tools for Continuous Improvement*.

RUN CHART

A run chart is a graphical tool that turns data into information. It is designed to show changes in a process measure over time. Variation in the data as well as trends and shifts in the process measure are easily seen. Suppose the following 15 data points were collected over time.

> 171, 156, 230, 147, 167, 183, 225, 190, 250, 245, 205, 210, 260, 270, 290

Table 5.9 Fifteen Consecutive Times
Between Unscheduled Maintenance Activities

If this data is plotted as a run chart or line graph where successive points are connected with straight lines, one can easily see a trend in the process measure. See Figure 5.12. Does this chart indicate process improvement?

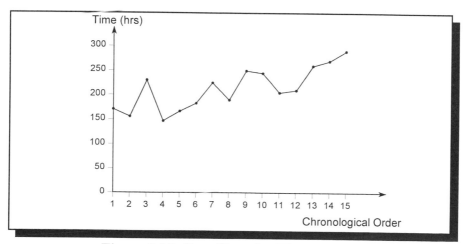

Figure 5.12 Run Chart for Time Between
Unscheduled Maintenance Activities

SCATTER DIAGRAM

A scatter diagram is a plot of points that shows the relationship between two variables. Suppose data on two different variables was collected as shown in Table 5.10.

Observation	Weight (lbs)	Mileage (mpg)
1	3000	18
2	2800	21
3	2100	32
4	2900	17
5	2400	31
6	3300	14
7	2700	21
8	3500	12
9	2500	23
10	3200	14

Table 5.10 Bivariate Data (Vehicle Weight vs Gas Mileage)

From this table, it is difficult to determine what kind of relationship exists between vehicle weight and mileage. However, if this data is plotted as a scatter diagram, where each variable represents an axis and each point represents an observation as shown in Figure 5.13, the relationship between the two variables becomes quite clear.

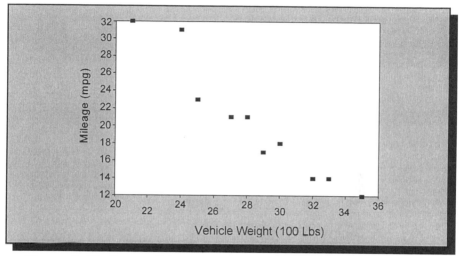

Figure 5.13 Scatter Diagram for Vehicle Weight vs Gas Mileage

If there appears to be a relationship between the two variables, as it does here, then they are said to be correlated. This figure shows a negative correlation, since as one variable (vehicle weight) gets larger, the other variable (mileage) tends to get smaller. Just because two variables may be strongly related does not mean that there exists a cause and effect relationship between the two. Further analysis using more advanced techniques (see Chapter 6) can help in determining a true cause and effect relationship.

The knowledge provided by the scatter diagram can be enhanced with the use of regression. This tool generates an equation that gives us an approximate relationship between the two variables.

For our example, the equation

$$mpg = 63.51 - 1.52 \ (weight)$$

is shown as the straight line in the scatter diagram in Figure 5.14. Now if we wish to predict the mileage of a 2600-pound car, the equation tells us:

$$mpg = 63.51 - 1.52(26) = 24.$$

Regression is a powerful tool that can be extended to show the relationship between many variables and a resulting dependent variable. For more information on scatter diagrams, correlation and regression analysis, see *Basic Statistics: Tools for Continuous Improvement.*

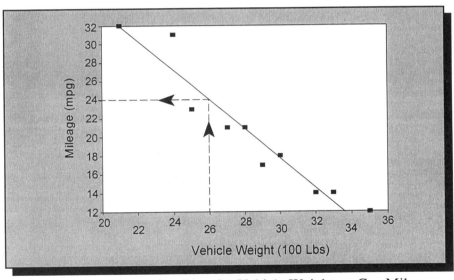

Figure 5.14 Regression Line for Vehicle Weight vs Gas Mileage

"Statistical thinking will one day be as necessary for efficient citizenship as the ability to read and write."

H.G. Wells

TEAMWORK

Effective teamwork is a critical factor in the success of Knowledge Based Management. It is in the team environment that all other tools are most effectively used. In this section, we present a framework for developing and maintaining good teams, the Team Improvement Process.

KEY ISSUES IN THE TEAM IMPROVEMENT PROCESS

1. **Goals**. Goals must be related to key customer satisfaction issues and key company issues. Each improvement team must establish who their internal and external customers are and make certain that the goals and objectives of the project are consistent with satisfying the needs of all customers along the chain to the ultimate end user customer. If the organization has specific goals then the improvement team aligns itself and its goals with those of the total organization.

2. **Complete Company Involvement**. The whole organization should be involved in the team process. This means that teams should be functioning in all areas of the organization: manufacturing, shipping, purchasing, accounting, design and development, maintenance, etc. In other words, all functional areas are looking for ways to improve. Each area has customer-focused measurements, customer-focused goals for these measurements, and teams to implement the improvement process by using the proper tools.

3. **Management Support**. There are several key ways that management can support the teams.

   ➤ Provide training in the use of the tools and in the team improvement process.

   ➤ Implement the recommended solutions, or communicate with the team why they cannot be implemented. *Never, never, never* ignore a team's recommendation. Address it promptly one way or another.

   ➤ Provide necessary resources. Management must respond immediately to all reasonable requests for resources.

   ➤ Guide project selection. This is done partly through having already established clear customer-focused goals and metrics for the team to use as a guide. In addition, major projects are often selected by a management team based on key customer and business issues, as well as COPQ.

   ➤ Participate on a team project as a <u>member</u>, not as someone running the show. In other words, all rank comes off at the start of the meeting.

   ➤ Make team projects a top priority, and don't interrupt team meetings or pull members out.

   ➤ Secure the team's environment by ensuring employees they will not be laid off if they improve a process to a point where jobs may be eliminated. Management must be committed to retraining and reassigning people to other job functions.

➤ Reward and recognize. There are many ways this can be done effectively.

- Publish, post, and present team success stories throughout the company.

- Provide dinners, tee shirts, etc., for participating on team projects.

- Improve working conditions. This may happen partly as an outcome of the team projects, but management should consider other improvements as necessary.

- Financial rewards for teams is a difficult area that should be addressed on a case-by-case basis. If the ROI from an improvement team can be precisely measured, the question of financial reward to the team becomes easier to answer. Raises, profit sharing, promotions and/or corporate shares should all be impacted positively by an individual's positive contribution to the team process.

➤ Set specific timelines. Projects that continue endlessly tend to flounder. Set up a timeline, follow it, and bring the project to closure.

➤ Coordinate the follow-up. Often teams will not be able to implement all facets of the improvement plan in the allotted time. Management must then appoint someone responsible to coordinate the follow up. This can be someone from the team, or it may be a small group. Determining ROI should be part of the follow-up.

➤ Review the project and conduct post mortems. This shows management support to the team process, generates feedback for the future, and provides closure.

4. Team Size. Five to eight is a good number, although as many as twelve may be necessary on some larger cross functional projects.

5. Team Make-up. Those responsible for the process, as well as key internal/external customers and suppliers, should be on the team. Many organizations have found it helpful to also include someone not directly involved with the process. This person can be very helpful in asking the question "Why are you doing that?"

6. Quick, Cheap, Simple. Teams should first look for changes that are quick, cheap, and simple. The process must be improved to its maximum efficiency and quality level before there is any consideration for capital equipment. Otherwise, the result will be to make more scrap and rework more quickly.   The biggest ROI in the improvement process comes from quick, cheap, simple changes.

7. Number of Projects.   One way to ensure that the quality improvement process is on-going is to set a goal for the number of major projects an organization completes each year. For example, in a large organization with a mature improvement process, 40 to 50 major projects each year is a feasible number. Top management should then review the progress of the teams at operations and/or business reviews. Management should review progress toward the number of projects as well as the success of the projects.

> Note: Not every project will be "successful" in monetary terms. Some may even be negative. But the bottom line is that some will be so successful that the overall impact should be a five to ten-fold ROI.

8. **Cultural impact will result in many collateral projects**. As an organization develops a critical mass of trained and experienced improvement team members, there should be many on-going unofficial or minor improvement projects occurring. These will be the result of workers in an organization working together to solve small problems that occur on a daily basis. Experienced teams will automatically perform root cause analysis and implement permanent solutions.

9. **How to implement the process**. The best way to train for and implement the Team Improvement Process is to use actual projects. These projects should be carefully selected to be of benefit to the organization and to be of educational value to the participants. Skilled facilitators from either internally trained persons or external consultants should lead the initial team projects. The goal is to eventually have enough internally trained facilitators and team leaders so the process will be self perpetuating.

10. **Change Management.** Process improvements are a result of changes accomplished by people. In order for a process to change, people must also change. Thus, a quality improvement management team needs a set of change management skills to facilitate process improvement. Change management is the tool that leverages the power of all of the other process improvement tools. Dr. Tom Cheek of Raytheon TI Systems summarizes some of the key issues of Change Management in Appendix C.

Chapter 6

ADVANCED TOOLS AND TECHNIQUES TO OBTAIN KNOWLEDGE

"An investment in knowledge always pays the best interest."

Benjamin Franklin

In this chapter we look at two important tools for gaining knowledge: Statistical Process Control (SPC) and Design of Experiments (DOE). These two tools are particularly important in the quest for knowledge since they have a track record of providing more information per dollar expended on data collection than almost any other quality improvement tool.

While this text has stressed the importance of gaining knowledge of our processes, products, people, and organizations, it is important to note that "perfect knowledge" means different things to different people. Executives and corporate staff view perfect knowledge as the goal of zero waste and absolute maximum profit. Their perspective is one of a journey along the process knowledge curve shown in Figure 6.1. Executives and corporate staff are concerned with the bottom line—profit. And, rightfully so. Profit is the metric by which we measure our success at the end of each fiscal year. But what about others in the organization?

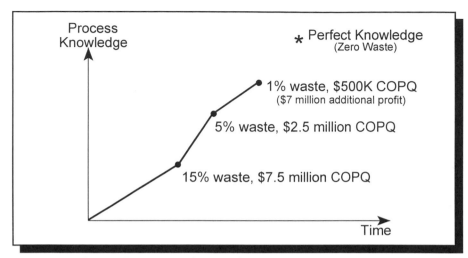

Figure 6.1 Executive's View of Process Knowledge

If we ask a quality manager to describe the quality of critical company processes, he/she will most likely use terms like C_{pk} or dpm that describe process capability. The quality manager has a different view of the process and thus a different view of increased process knowledge. See Figure 6.2.

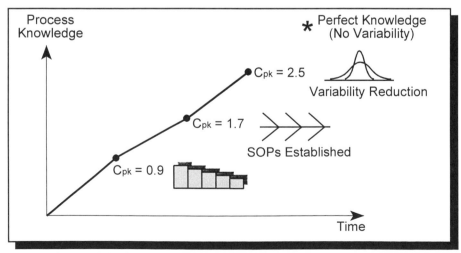

Figure 6.2 Quality Manager's View of Process Knowledge

Another possible view is that of the practitioner. This is the person closest to the process and the one who is concerned with *how* the process works. Often, it is difficult to tie this view to that of management. Some practitioners simply want to model the process mathematically or be able to predict the outcome of the process using sophisticated analysis tools. This view of process knowledge is depicted below.

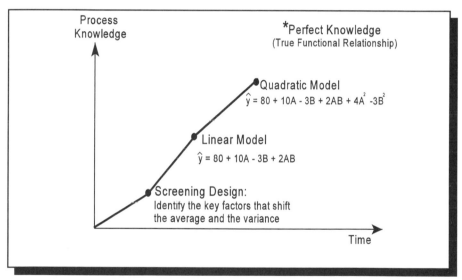

Figure 6.3 Practitioner's View of Process Knowledge

All of these views of process knowledge are valid! They are from different perspectives but they translate to the same thing. The practitioner's much more detailed, quantitative understanding of the process should enable the quality manager to report fewer defects and less waste, which should excite the corporate staff with increased profits.

This chapter addresses the methods of building process knowledge quantitatively, by collecting data, predicting outcomes, and measuring success. SPC and DOE can help accomplish these tasks so that everyone can move up his/her own process knowledge curve.

STATISTICAL PROCESS CONTROL (SPC)

Statistical Process Control (SPC) is actually a collection of tools used to study the behavior of a process over time. This set of tools, which is mostly statistical in nature, consists of many of the simple tools presented in Chapter 5, such as histograms, Pareto charts, cause and effect diagrams, and process flow diagrams. However, the SPC tool that yields the greatest power is the control chart. Hence, our brief excursion into SPC in this chapter will focus on this tool. In using SPC, we collect data from a process and use that data to determine the "health" of the process. In effect, we are listening to what the process has to say. Is it in control? Is it out of control? Is it improving or getting worse?

In evaluating control charts, we have one of two situations that could exist: (A) the process is in control or (B) the process is out of control. The theory behind SPC requires that we accept A unless sufficient evidence exists to prove B. In other words, we will look for symptoms of an out-of-control process. Figure 6.4 shows a control chart broken up into zones. If the process is in control and data is collected for a reasonable amount of time, we expect a certain percentage of points to fall into each zone.

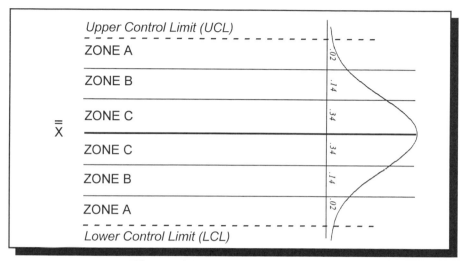

Figure 6.4 Control Chart Zones

Using this information, statisticians developed several rules for detecting out-of-control processes. The rules listed in Table 6.1 are some of the symptoms that indicate when a special cause is affecting the process. These are not the only symptoms that may occur but they are some of the most common.

- One or more points outside the control limits
- 7 consecutive points on one side of the centerline
- 7 consecutive increasing or decreasing intervals
- 2 out of 3 consecutive points in a specific zone A or beyond
- 4 out of 5 consecutive points in a specific zone B or beyond
- 14 consecutive points that alternate up or down
- 14 consecutive points in either zone C

Table 6.1 Symptoms of an Out-of-Control Process

Let's look at an interesting example from *Basic Statistics: Tools for Continuous Improvement* (Air Academy Press) to illustrate the power of SPC.

A nuclear power plant uses deuterium oxide (heavy water) to moderate the neutrons produced during the fission process. The heat released by fission is removed from the reactor core by circulating heavy water through the core. To study and control the water usage, meters record the water usage at each of four pumps at 30-minute intervals. The four readings are collected and an average ($\bar{x}$) and a range (R) are calculated for each set of four readings. The $\bar{x}$-R charts in Figures 6.5 and 6.6 show the results of the initial readings of 25 subgroups.

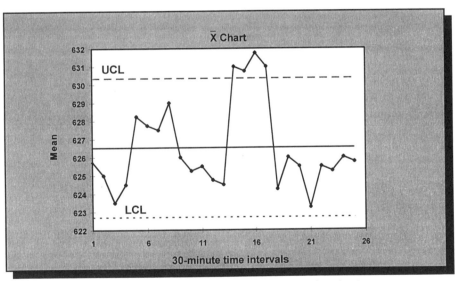

Figure 6.5 $\bar{x}$ Chart (Before Investigation)

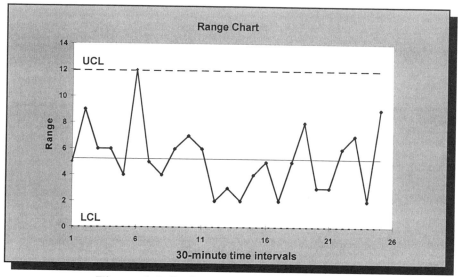

Figure 6.6 R Chart (Before Investigation)

The control limits are constructed in such a manner that we expect approximately 99.7% of all data points to fall between them. Therefore, it is unlikely that point number 6 on the range chart and points 14-17 on the x̄ chart are due to chance alone.

In this case, an investigation to find the special causes for these out-of-control symptoms revealed that the electrical power was cut off for several minutes in the vicinity of one of the pumps just prior to the collection of data for subgroup 6. An operator had cut the power to work on a fuse box and did not realize that this box also controlled the power to the pump. Proper operator training should remove this special source of variability.

When investigating the cause for the out-of-control points on the x̄ chart, quality personnel found that a thermostat monitoring the temperature of the heavy water was replaced shortly before the data was collected. It turned out that the thermostat was not properly calibrated, leading to an increase in the amount of fresh heavy water pumped into the reactor core. A further check on the lot of thermostats from which this one was selected indicates that the entire lot was improperly calibrated. This led to a requirement that the thermostat vendor must chart his calibration process and demonstrate a stable, predictable process.

Once the offending data points were removed (since they were a result of special causes) the control charts appeared as shown in Figures 6.7 and 6.8:

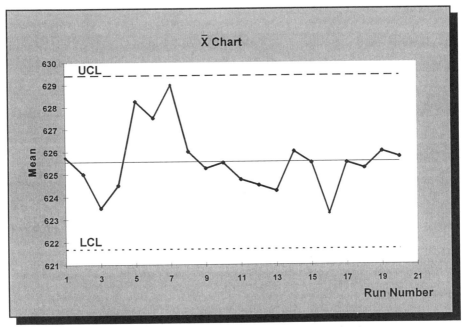

Figure 6.7 x̄ Chart (After Investigation)

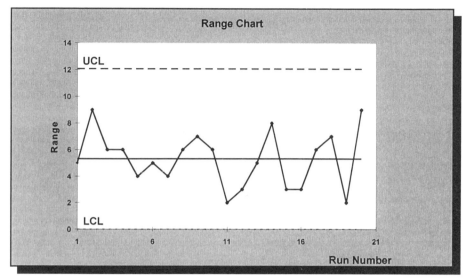

Figure 6.8 R Chart (After Investigation)

These charts now reflect a stable process. At this time, data would continue to be collected, and the operators would again keep looking for special causes of variation—evidence to show that the process is out of control.

SPC is not just a tool for technical applications. There are many uses of SPC in management and the service industry. Below is an example that demonstrates the power of SPC in a management environment.

The manager of an accounts payable department in a large corporation faced a serious crisis. This department was responsible for receiving, validating, and paying all the invoices the corporation received from its vendors. The manager had received numerous calls from vendors complaining that their invoices were not being paid within thirty days of receipt in accordance with the terms of their contracts. The manager was also under pressure from the corporate comptroller not to pay any invoices until they were within ten days of their due date.

Faced with this set of seemingly conflicting demands, the manager decided to take a closer look at the accounts payable process. Five invoices were randomly selected every day for two weeks (ten working days). The number of days required to receive, validate, and pay these invoices were recorded and plotted on the charts on Figures 6.9 and 6.10. Figure 6.9 shows the average processing time per day over the ten-day period. This is called an x̄ Chart because each point plotted is an average of (in this case) five individual invoice processing times. The average of all 50 invoice processing times, sometimes called the grand average, is the centerline (approximately 27.5 days). Figure 6.10 is called a Range Chart because each point plotted represents the range (largest value minus smallest value) of that day's processing times.

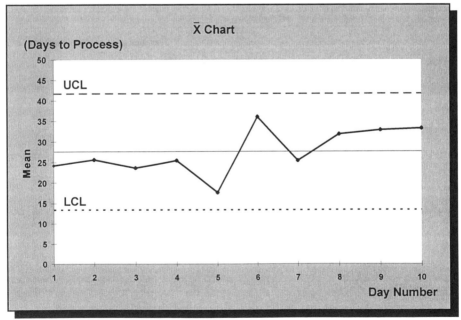

Figure 6.9 x̄ Chart

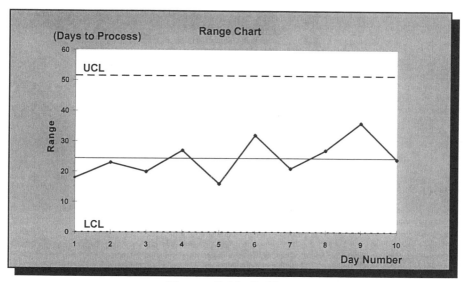

Figure 6.10 R Chart

The charts indicate that the process was in control; however, the manager was aware that he was not meeting vendor and corporate requirements. When he examined individual invoices, he found that only about one third (17 of 50) of those sampled conformed to both sets of requirements.

Upon further examination of the control charts, we see that the average time to process an invoice is well within the 20 to 30 day window. However, the range chart shows that the variability is much too high. The average range of 24.4 days indicates that although the average time to process an invoice conforms to standards, there will be many individual invoices that do not. What is happening is shown graphically in Figure 6.11, where it is seen that a high proportion of the invoice processing times do not fall within the desired window.

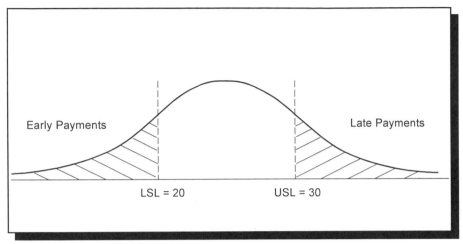

Figure 6.11 Process Capability

Thus, the manager was able to identify the problem. There is too much variability in the process. Further work by his employees in examining process flow diagrams and establishing standard operating procedures would allow him to remove this variability.

This example illustrates the difference between control limits and specification limits. The process was in control since only natural variability was present. However, the process was not capable. That is, it did not meet specifications. In this case the control chart is still useful in finding the problems in meeting the specifications—too much natural variability.

"*Variability is like a virus. Each process can infect the one it touches, including the management of the process. Infected processes are noisy and produce noisy meetings.*"

Myron Tribus

One of the most common applications of SPC is in an area called Gage Capability. Variability in any process arises from a variety of sources: machine, operator, materials, environment, methodology, and measurement, to name a few. The focus of a Gage Capability study is on the measurement system or instrument (i.e., gage or test equipment). Its purpose is to assess how much variation is associated with the measurement system and to compare it to the total process variation. Understanding and quantifying this measurement error is an important aspect that is often overlooked when charting and improving a process. The following example provides a brief illustration.

A quality improvement team interested in assessing the measurement capability of an instrument used to measure the thickness of a printed wire board conducted the following gage study. To assess the ability of the instrument to repeatedly measure board thickness, a process operator took 30 measurements randomly throughout the day, always using the same board, the same instrument, and measuring at the same place on the board every time. Figure 6.12 shows the variability in the 30 measurements. Except for the one point which exceeds the upper control limit (UCL), the measurements tend to fall within a 5-mil range. The outlying point needs to be investigated because such an outlier is not likely to have occurred as part of the natural variation in the measurement system. In fact, the cause for such an outlier can usually be traced to one of the following:

   a) Inadequate SOPs,
   b) Failure to follow SOPs, or
   c) Noise factors.

The underlying cause of this outlier needs to be identified and removed from the measurement system in order to prevent future occurrences.

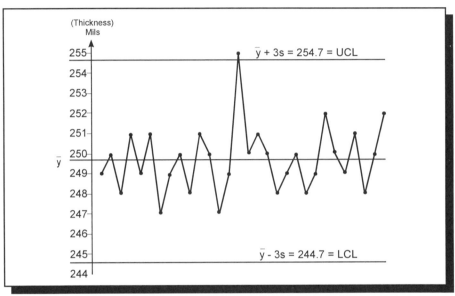

Figure 6.12 30 Repeated, Random Measurements of Board Thickness

A Rule of Thumb commonly used to determine measurement system capability is:

$$\frac{\text{Measurement System Standard Deviation}}{\text{Total Process Standard Deviation}} < .10$$

If the variability in the measurement system itself is large, it can mask legitimate variance reduction efforts and prevent knowledge gaining activities from occurring. For more information on Gage Capability, reference *Basic Statistics: Tools for Continuous Improvement*.

DESIGN OF EXPERIMENTS (DOE)

While SPC can be thought of as "listening to the voice of the process," DOE can be thought of as "interrogating the process." DOE is possibly the single most powerful tool in gaining process knowledge and it is fast becoming a competitive necessity. With proper training, engineers, scientists, and technicians around the world are using DOE more and more every day to achieve monumental increases in process knowledge. The result: decreased product development time, scrap and rework, and increased profit. The following example will illustrate the way DOE works and its implications for increased process knowledge.

This example involves a chemical analysis process. Problems occurred in trying to hit the target rate of 1620. In fact, when data was collected, the process capability was determined to be as shown in Figure 6.13.

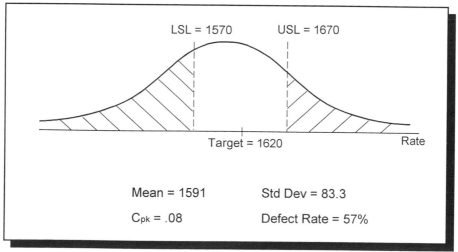

Figure 6.13 Process Capability (Before Experimentation)

As you can see, this is not a good process. The first step in improving this process is to define the process with a complete process flow and cause and effect diagram. The IPO diagram in Figure 6.14 lists the factors that were thought to have some influence on the output. These factors were derived from a brainstorming session involving many of the personnel that work on the process.

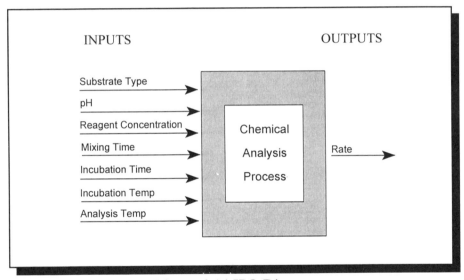

Figure 6.14 IPO Diagram

To determine the precise effect of each factor on the output mean and standard deviation, team members decided to conduct an experiment. They decided to test each factor at two levels (settings) and to use a structured testing approach (i.e., DOE).

Next, high and low settings had to be chosen for each factor in the experiment. These settings were selected through group discussions. They represent changes around nominal levels of the input factors. See Table 6.2.

FACTOR	NAME	LOW (-1)	HIGH (+1)
A	Substrate Type	Vendor A_1	Vendor A_2
B	pH	4.5	7.5
C	Reagent Concentration	2%	5%
D	Mixing Time	1	5
E	Incubation Time	1	5
F	Incubation Temperature	100	120
G	Analysis Temperature	80	100

Table 6.2 Factors and Levels

The design matrix in Table 6.3 gives the settings for this experiment. Each row represents an experimental run. For example, the first row shows that all factors were set at their "low" (-1) values. The four response values (Y1, Y2, Y3, and Y4) are the recorded output values from four tests per experimental run. Notice in columns 1 through 7 that each factor is run six times at the "low" setting and six times at the "high" setting. Also notice that when factor A is set at the "low," all of the other factors are balanced, half at the "low" and half at the "high." This property is referred to as *orthogonality*. For more information, refer to the book *Understanding Industrial Designed Experiments*.

Col. #	1	2	3	4	5	6	7	Rate			
Row #	A	B	C	D	E	F	G	Y1	Y2	Y3	Y4
1	-1	-1	-1	-1	-1	-1	-1	532.4	460.1	646.7	501.0
2	-1	-1	-1	-1	-1	1	1	647.4	435.1	624.0	493.8
3	-1	-1	1	1	1	-1	-1	1270.8	1356.3	1198.6	1248.0
4	-1	1	-1	1	1	-1	1	895.5	966.8	837.8	1043.3
5	-1	1	1	-1	1	1	-1	1572.1	1699.9	1693.4	1518.9
6	-1	1	1	1	-1	-1	1	1584.7	1395.1	1334.1	1388.7
7	1	-1	1	1	-1	1	1	1092.8	1100.8	1049.6	1072.7
8	1	-1	-1	1	1	1	-1	1205.7	1235.8	1224.0	1253.2
9	1	-1	1	-1	1	1	-1	694.5	681.5	748.7	643.5
10	1	1	1	1	-1	-1	1	1423.2	1461.3	1411.2	1416.7
11	1	1	-1	-1	-1	1	-1	806.9	849.6	799.4	773.2
12	1	1	-1	-1	1	-1	1	950.7	966.5	923.3	957.4

Table 6.3 Screening Design Matrix

This design property (orthogonality) allows us to measure the effects of each factor independently of the others and has a knowledge gaining multiplier effect over any other experimentation strategy. If we were to look at all combinations of these factors at two levels, we would need a matrix with 128 (2^7) rows. The 12-run design used and shown here is much more efficient, and we are still able to identify factors that shift the average and factors that affect variability. The results of the experiment can be analyzed graphically from Figures 6.15 and 6.16.

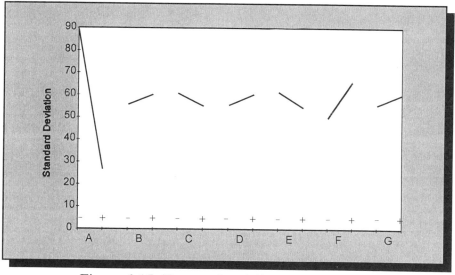

Figure 6.15 Factors that Affect the Variability

From Figure 6.15, we see that factor A (substrate type) stands out (because of the steep slope) as a significant factor for decreasing variability. In fact, the plot shows that when A is set at the "high" (+ setting), variability is reduced significantly. This means that Vendor A_2's substrate produces significantly less variability in the output than does Vendor A_1's substrate.

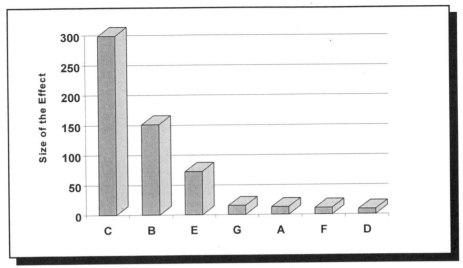

Figure 6.16 Factors that Affect the Average

In Figure 6.16, we also see that factors C, B, and E have the largest effects, respectively, on the average response. The 12-run experiment just performed is called a "screening design." It has literally screened out one factor (substrate type) as significant for reducing variability and three other factors (reagent concentration, pH, and incubation time) as significantly affecting the average response. We will use this information to set up another experiment designed to give us even more information.

The next step is to conduct a "modeling" experiment where only the three factors known to have the largest effect on the average response are considered. Factor A will be set at the high value (substrate from vendor A_2) to minimize variability and factors D, F, and G will be set at their most economical settings since these have no apparent effect on either the average response or the variability. Factors B (pH), C (reagent concentration), and E (incubation time) are varied again, at their low and high values. Table 6.4 shows the results of the new "modeling" experiment.

Column #	1	2	3						
Row #	pH (B)	REA CONC (C)	ITIME (E)		Y1	Y2	Y3	Y4	Y5
1	4.5	2	1		516.0760	585.8470	589.3176	537.1530	604.7294
2	4.5	2	5		699.1882	695.9177	735.2235	688.1882	648.0823
3	4.5	5	1		1042.4710	1119.2820	1057.3530	1090.8940	1047.5060
4	4.5	5	5		1260.5180	1257.2000	1215.6000	1176.6470	1180.9410
5	7.5	2	1		809.5647	767.4000	745.0823	793.4353	820.7411
6	7.5	2	5		898.1294	991.6824	954.8941	973.3412	937.1530
7	7.5	5	1		1425.0940	1502.2590	1479.5650	1492.3060	1478.4470
8	7.5	5	5		1571.5650	1665.5290	1637.3650	1677.4820	1658.6350

Table 6.4 Modeling Design Matrix

The difference between this experiment and the earlier one is that this one allows us to build a model—an equation that explains the relationship between the input factors and the resulting output (rate). The experiment given above yields the following equation (computer output not shown—see the book *Understanding Industrial Designed Experiments*):

$$\text{Rate} = 1050 + 163.2\,B + 301.1\,C + 75.5\,E + 43.7\,B*C$$

This equation predicts the rate at various settings of B, C and E where B, C and E take on "coded" values (i.e., values from -1 to +1). That is, when B is set at +1 in the equation, it corresponds to a pH of 7.5. When C is set at +1, it means that reagent concentration is "high" at a value of 5. Using software to investigate the effect of various settings of the input factors, we can find the optimal settings for factors B, C, and E to give a target rate of 1620. Also, recall that in the screening experiment, factor A affected variability. The optimal settings are given in Table 6.5. The other factors may be set at their most economical settings.

FACTOR	NAME	Optimal
A	Substrate Type	Vendor A_2
B	pH	7.5
C	Reagent Concentration	5%
E	Incubation Time	4.6

Table 6.5 Optimal Settings

When we go into production we get the following results:

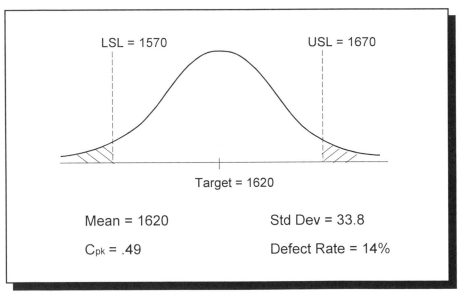

Figure 6.17 Process Capability (After Experimentation)

We can see that we made a significant improvement. From 57% defects down to 14%. This, by itself, represents a remarkable savings. But is the process good enough? A 14% defect rate is still high. We might be inclined to think that DOE gave us some useful results but it really didn't solve the entire problem. Let's now think in terms of *process knowledge*. What have we *learned* about this chemical process?

The answer: "A lot!" We know that hitting a target is not a problem. We can do this by controlling three variables. Our primary concern is variation. We need to decrease variation in order to decrease our defect rate. What affects variability? Substrate type! We now know that there is something different in the substrates (from vendors A_1 and A_2) that is causing the variability to change. By further investigating the substrates, we may be able to obtain more knowledge that will yield even less variability.

Knowledge leading to large reductions in variation is critical to reducing waste. Such knowledge, as shown in the prior example, can only be obtained efficiently through the use of properly designed experiments.

> "There are three principal means of acquiring knowledge: observation of nature, reflection, and experimentation. Observation collects facts; reflection combines them; and experimentation verifies the result of that combination. Our observation of nature must be diligent; our reflection profound; and our experimentation exact. We rarely see these three means combined; and for this reason, creative geniuses are not common."

Denis Diderot

SUMMARY

SPC and DOE are two of the most important tools available to the person who is serious about gaining process knowledge. When viewed as tools that yield information, they become crucial to a successful Knowledge Based Management approach. Furthermore, they tell us where opportunities for improvement exist and where to devote our resources for maximum return on investment. They also provide measurements of process performance and predictability. When this increase in knowledge takes place for the practitioners (see Figure 6.3), there is a corresponding increase in quality (see Figure 6.2) and increase in profits (see Figure 6.1).

Chapter 7

KBM: A MODERN QUALITY IMPROVEMENT PARADIGM

*"If we would have new knowledge,
we must get a whole world of new questions."*

Susanne K. Langer

Around the world all types of organizations have wrestled with how to make their products, services, and associated process performance better, faster, and at lower cost. Boards of Directors, CEOs, Vice Presidents, directors, middle managers, and all employees in general should realize that better, faster, lower cost products, services and processes reflect true quality improvement which generates real return on investment and results in increased job security. Many people do realize this but still struggle to make it happen.

The problem in our organizations is *how* to make it happen. Past attempts focused on reorganizing or chasing the "fad of the month." The puzzle appears to be getting more complicated and can cause people to give up in frustration.

"...we tend to meet any new situation by reorganizing, and a wonderful method it can be for creating the illusion of progress while producing confusion, inefficiency and demoralization."

Petronius Arbitar - 66 A.D.

The height of frustration comes with mandated or regulated supplier quality improvement requirements. For international trade it's ISO-9000; for supplying the U.S. automotive giants (GM, Ford and Chrysler) it's QS-9000; for Boeing suppliers it's D1-9000; in the pharmaceutical and medical device industry it's the FDA's Process Validation; for the electronics industry it's Process Characterization; and for Motorola suppliers it's Quality Systems Review (QSR). Many other industries have similar requirements or use the Malcolm Baldrige criteria for self evaluation.

The intent of these mandated or regulated supplier quality improvement requirements is to ensure 1) the customers get better, faster and lower cost products and services and 2) the suppliers become more profitable. However, the process of meeting regulated requirements often becomes little more than a "paperwork exercise." Customers may not actually see improved products and services, and suppliers realize little or no return on their investment. This paradigm of letting regulations drive quality improvement is like the old saying, "We've put the cart before the horse!" See Figure 7.1.

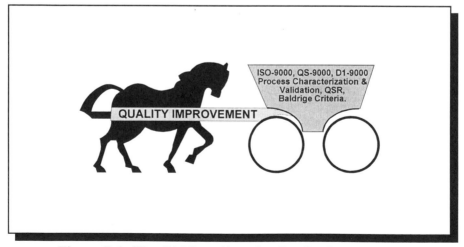

Figure 7.1 The Old Paradigm for Quality Improvement

The Knowledge Based Management (KBM) paradigm has the cart and horse hitched together in a way that will get us safely and efficiently down the road to success. See Figure 7.2.

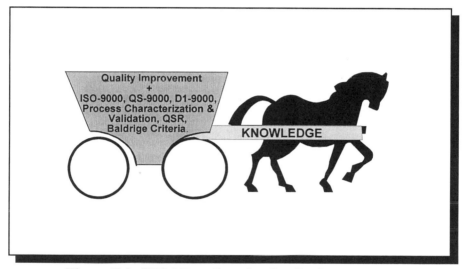

Figure 7.2 KBM Paradigm for Quality Improvement

As discussed in the previous chapters, knowledge is the basic building block and foundation for making good decisions, which allows quality improvement to take place. If we truly have knowledge, then we should be able to answer pertinent questions. The practice of KBM requires that managers can satisfactorily answer the questions discussed in Chapter 3. These questions are also listed in Appendix A so the reader can easily access them for future reference.

"Not knowing the difference between opinion and fact makes it difficult to make good decisions."

Marilyn Vos Savant

In a KBM environment, managers will ask their people the questions discussed in Chapter 4. These questions, along with the tools needed to answer each question, are presented in Appendix B so the reader can easily access them for future reference. An effective manager will be well versed in the change management skills presented in Appendix C and will also ensure that his/her people have been successfully trained in the best tools and techniques to answer these questions. The ability to answer these questions is the key to generating the knowledge that is the foundation of a KBM approach and that leads to the desired results. See Figure 7.3.

> *"Asking questions and looking for answers without fear is how true solutions are found."*

Lyell Jennings
Focused Quality

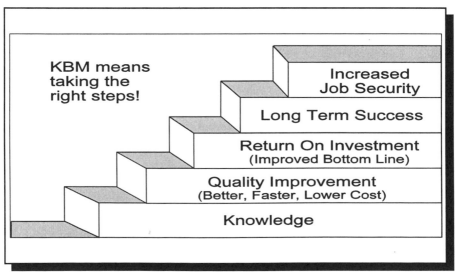

Figure 7.3 KBM Gets the Desired Results

When we implement a KBM approach to quality improvement, it should be obvious that the reason we're doing it is for the security of our company and ourselves. If we can't see the personal benefits of what we're doing, it's difficult to get motivated. Consequently, an ISO-9000, QS-9000, or Process Validation, etc., motivated approach to quality improvement breeds an air of "we're doing this for our customer— but we don't know why." No wonder there is a lot of frustration in organizations whose management is not KBM-oriented.

We need to make it clear that the authors are not opposed to supplier quality requirements such as ISO-9000, QS-9000, D1-9000, Process Validation, Process Characterization, QSR, and the Baldrige Criteria. Rather, it is a question of what is truly driving our efforts. If we start with a KBM approach and generate knowledge throughout the organization, compliance with any supplier requirements should be little more than a repackaging of the knowledge we have already accumulated.

By now we hope the message is clear. Certainly, some readers and many non-readers will continue thinking along the lines of the old paradigm. In our minds, it's just a matter of time before everyone will have to consider the following: what happens when all the suppliers in a specific industry have shuffled the paperwork to present an appearance of compliance with supplier requirements? That is, what happens when all suppliers have "filled the square for ISO-9000, etc?" Now, how do we choose? Won't we eventually have to migrate to a paradigm based on "best valued products and services" in choosing our suppliers? This is the focus of a KBM approach. Why not start now? Figure 7.4 summarizes our KBM philosophy and how the pieces of the quality improvement puzzle fit together to build success.

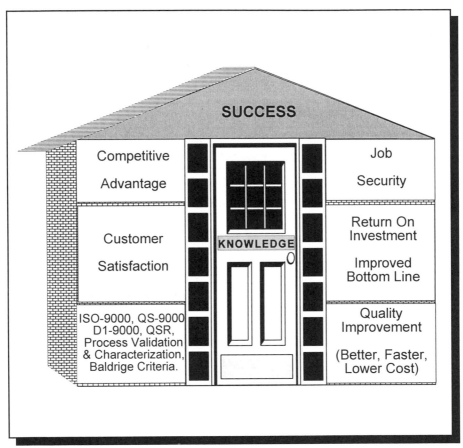

Figure 7.4 Summary of a KBM Philosophy: A House of Success

"*By wisdom a house is built,
and through understanding it is established;
through knowledge its rooms are filled with
rare and beautiful treasures.*"

Prov 24:3-4

How will we know if KBM is working for us? Implementing KBM implies that we have posted the proper scorecard. The scorecard must be comprehensive, balanced, complete, and reflect improvement. If your company is committed to giving KBM a chance to work, Question 12 in Appendix A (Questions Managers Need to Answer) is critical: *What metrics are you evaluated on that relate to quality issues? Are you held accountable for these metrics? What are the specific improvement goals for these metrics?* To satisfactorily answer these questions, we will need to spend a great deal of time completing the scorecard which is shown in Table 7.1. Some items for your consideration have been inserted in each category to assist you in filling out the scorecard. To make KBM happen, complete the scorecard, post it in a weekly staff meeting, set stretch goals, hold people accountable, and coach them through the other aspects of KBM to get a winning score.

> *"If you are not keeping score,*
> *you are just practicing."*

Vince Lombardi

	Performance (Better)	Schedule (Faster)	Cost (Lower Cost)
Organization	- Stock price - Market share - Organizational Climate	- Milestones - Timelines - Reaction Time	- Operational Cost - Advertising Cost - Materials Cost - Taxes - Budgets - Profits
Product	- Meeting Customer Needs - Customer Complaints - Reliability - Availability	- Development Time - Design Time - Design Changes	- Development Cost - Design Cost - Product Price - Lifecycle Cost - Cost of Poor Quality - Profit Margin
Process	- Defect Rate - C_{pk} - Customer Complaints	- Process Development Time - Down Time - Daily Production Rate	- Manufacturing Cost - Cost of Poor Quality
People	- Product Rate - Defect Rate - Safety Violation Rate - Absenteeism - Suggestion Rate	- Training Time - Rehabilitation Time - Learning Curve Time	- Turnover Rate - Training Cost - Legal Costs - Absentee Costs - Ergonomic Costs - Benefit Costs

Table 7.1 KBM Scorecard

"Knowledge is what we get when an observer, preferably a trained observer, provides us with a copy of reality that we can all recognize."

Christopher Lasch

In summary, Knowledge Based Management means getting back to the basics. Precise, detailed knowledge about our processes, products, people, and organization provide the building blocks for survival and beyond. We challenge each reader to get back to the basics and begin to build the infrastructure needed to make our systems and operations stable, predictable, and successful. Nothing truly worthwhile is ever easy, but Knowledge Based Management can provide the philosophy, strategy, and tools to make it happen. The challenge is yours. Will you accept it?

> *"Even supposing knowledge to be easily attainable, more people would be content to be ignorant than would take even a little trouble to acquire it."*

Samuel Johnson

QUALITY IMPROVEMENT ORIENTED QUESTIONS MANAGERS NEED TO ANSWER!

1. What is your product or service and who are your customers?

2. What perception do your customers have of your product or service? How do you know?

3. Do you believe quality issues are important to your company? Why? Which ones?

4. What is the company's current share of the total market? Can quality improvement efforts assist you in increasing the market share and/or increasing profits? How?

5. Are you actively pursuing quality improvement in your areas of responsibility? How?

6. How many hours (days) per week (month) do you currently have scheduled (on your calendar) that are devoted strictly to quality issues?

7. How often per week (month) do you solicit feedback from the people you manage? What kind of feedback do you solicit? What do you do with the feedback?

(Continued on next page)

Quality Improvement Oriented Questions
Managers Need to Answer!

8. What are the right quality-oriented questions managers need to ask their people? What methods or tools can be used to answer them?

9. Are your people trained to successfully use the best quality improvement tools? What is your Return On Investment (ROI) from the training?

10. Do you have a standard procedure for documenting quality improvement efforts? What is it?

11. What barriers do your people face when trying to do quality improvement? What are you doing to remove these barriers?

12. What metrics are you evaluated on that relate to quality issues? Are you held accountable for these metrics? What are the specific improvement goals for these metrics?

13. How much waste does your company have? That is, what (in dollars) is the company's Cost Of Poor Quality (COPQ)? How much of the total waste is your area responsible for?

14. One year from now what evidence will you have to show that you made a difference?

Quality Improvement Oriented Questions
Managers Need to Answer!

Appendix B

1. What processes (activities) are you responsible for? Who is the owner of these processes? Who are the team members? How well does the team work together?

    Tools and Techniques Used to Answer These Questions:
    - *Communication*
    - *Teamwork*
    - *Common Sense*

2. Which processes have the highest priority for improvement? How did you come to this conclusion? Where is the data that led to this conclusion?

    Tools and Techniques Used to Answer These Questions:
    - *Cost of Poor Quality Analysis*
    - *Pareto Chart*
    - *Teamwork*
    - *Common Sense*

For those processes to be improved,

3.   How is the process performed?

Tools and Techniques Used to Answer This Question:
- *Process Flow Diagram*
- *Input-Process-Output (IPO) Diagram*
- *Teamwork*
- *Common Sense*

4.   What are your process performance measures? Why?   How accurate and precise is your measurement system?

Tools and Techniques Used to Answer These Questions:
- *QFD (to determine measures of performance related to customer needs)*
- *Gage Capability (to determine measurement system accuracy and precision)*
- *Teamwork*
- *Common Sense*

5. What are the customer driven specifications for all
    of your performance measures? How good or bad
    is the current performance? Show me the data.
    What are the improvement goals for the process?

    Tools and Techniques Used to Answer These Questions:
    - *QFD*
    - *Benchmarking*
    - *Control Charts*
    - *Capability Study (C_{pk})*
    - *Yield Analysis*
    - *Teamwork*
    - *Common Sense*

6. What are all the sources of variability in the
    process? Show me what they are.

    Tools and Techniques Used to Answer This Question:
    - *Cause and Effect (Fishbone or Ishikawa)
      Diagram*
    - *Failure Mode and Effects Analysis (FMEA)*
    - *Fault Tree Analysis (FTA)*
    - *Teamwork*
    - *Common Sense*

7. Which sources of variability do you control? How do you control them and what is your method of documentation?

    Tools and Techniques Used to Answer This Question:
    *   *Cause and Effect (Fishbone or Ishikawa) Diagram*
    *   *Teamwork*
    *   *Common Sense*

8. Are any of the sources of variability supplier-dependent? If so, what are they, who is the supplier, and what are we doing about it?

    Tools and Techniques Used to Answer These Questions:
    *   *Histogram*
    *   *Run Chart*
    *   *Control Chart*
    *   *Design of Experiments (DOE)*
    *   *Brainstorming*
    *   *Teamwork*
    *   *Common Sense*

9. What are the key variables that affect the average and variation of the measures of performance? How do you know this? Show me the data.

   Tools and Techniques Used to Answer These Questions:
   - *Design of Experiments (DOE)*
   - *Historical Data Modeling (Regression Analysis)*
   - *Teamwork*
   - *Common Sense*

10. What are the relationships between the measures of performance and the key variables? Do any key variables interact? How do you know for sure? Show me the data.

    Tools and Techniques Used to Answer These Questions:
    - *Design of Experiments (DOE)*
    - *Historical Data Modeling (Regression Analysis)*
    - *Teamwork*
    - *Common Sense*

11. What setting for the key variables will optimize the measures of performance? How do you know this? Show me the data.

Tools and Techniques Used to Answer These Questions:
- *Design of Experiments (DOE)*
- *Historical Data Modeling (Regression Analysis)*
- *Teamwork*
- *Common Sense*

12. For the optimal settings of the key variables, what kind of variability exists in the performance measures? How do you know? Show me the data.

Tools and Techniques Used to Answer These Questions:
- *Design of Experiments (DOE)*
- *Statistical Process Control (SPC)*
- *Capability Study (C_{pk})*
- *Teamwork*
- *Common Sense*

13. How much improvement has the process shown in the past 6 months? How do you know this? Show me the data.

Tools and Techniques Used to Answer These Questions:
- *Run Chart*
- *Control Chart*
- *COPQ Analysis*
- *Teamwork*
- *Common Sense*

14. How much time and/or money have your efforts saved or generated for the company? How did you document all of your efforts? Show me the data.

Tools and Techniques Used to Answer These Questions:
- *Run Chart*
- *Control Chart*
- *Correlation Studies*
- *Teamwork*
- *Common Sense*

Appendix C

CHANGE MANAGEMENT

Knowledge Based Management is getting the desired results through changing, adopting, and modifying the existing processes and procedures of both people and organizations. These changes are always accomplished by people; if people are not motivated to change, change will not occur. From our experience, the human side of the change process can be more complicated and confusing than the technical side of change. Hence, knowledge of how people react and cope with change is critical in the success of any organization's implementation strategy. The universal human phenomenon of resistance to change must be managed in order to achieve a profitable and long-lasting quality improvement initiative. The purpose of this appendix is not to present an in-depth study of change management. Rather, we will propose that the following questions be considered by those who are serious about generating positive change that leads to better, faster, and lower cost products and services.

Consider the following questions that must be addressed for successful change to take place.

Critical Questions to Consider in Order to Manage Change

1. What are the normal reactions to change?

Psychologists suggest that during a major change in an individual's life certain trends in human behavior take place. These behaviors generally follow a certain pattern. This pattern is depicted in

Figure C.1 which illustrates the natural and normal behavior of individuals progressing through the change process.

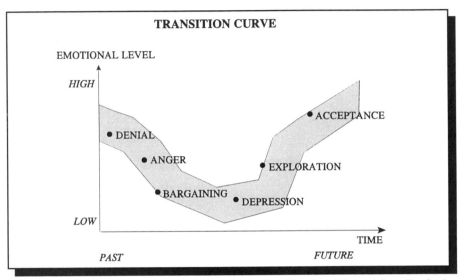

Figure C.1 Levels of Emotional Intensity During Transition Period

As shown, there are a number of different phases or stages that an individual will go through as change takes place. These different phases can usually be identified by listening to comments that people make. For example,

    1.   Denial — "This can't be happening." or "I don't believe this."

    2.   Anger —"I don't want to, I don't have to, and you can't make me."

    3.   Bargaining — "Maybe we can work something out."

    4.   Depression —"I don't feel good. I can't deal with this right now."

5.   Exploration — "How about if we try this _____."

6.   Acceptance — "Thanks, I really needed that."

Note from the transition curve, there is not a distinctive separation between phases and each phase has a range of emotional intensity. Consider for example, the case of traumatic loss. The stages and levels of emotional intensity vary from an initial stage of denial to the final stage of acceptance; with steps such as anger, bargaining, depression, and exploration sandwiched between denial and acceptance. The transition curve shown can be used as a roadmap. This roadmap can help us understand what we and others go through when dealing with a major change, even though it may not be a traumatic change. In a less traumatic change, an individual may minimize certain steps or move through the various phases quickly—moving through anger in a short period of time and virtually skipping bargaining and depression. Regardless, an individual needs some time to change as they progress through these natural phases. The amount of time required to change will vary depending on the individual and how they are managed. In other words, if we understand where an individual is in the change process we can modify how we interface with them to help speed up the process.

2.   Why do people resist change?

A variety of reasons exist for people to resist change in the workplace. Some people resist change due to their large investment of time and effort in the "status quo." For example, people who have worked hard for many years to obtain a powerful position could have the most to lose both financially and emotionally. Hence, they have the strongest motivation to maintain the "status quo." If they perceive change as something that decreases their importance or status, they will likely oppose it overtly or covertly.

Another reason to resist change is the "fear of the unknown." This fear is caused by the omnipresent human desire for predictability and sense of control over one's life. Leaving the known for something new is inherently unsettling and involves facing many uncertainties and risks. Fear of any type is a very powerful force and is difficult to overcome.

Tradition and "nostalgia" may also arouse strong emotions, such as: resistance to changing something that is tied to past successes, changing things that have major emotional importance, or abandoning original and long-standing organizational core concepts. From a broader perspective, major resistance is often linked to the pleasant memories of the past and an unwillingness to give them up.

Another reason to resist change might simply be described as pride. Suppose someone interprets the need for change to imply that they failed in the past. In this case, it is very possible for pride to override logical thinking and resistance to change sets in. From a slightly different angle, a person can resist change if they despise who or what the change represents. For example, if a person has become nauseated with years of listening to "quality this" and "quality that" they may get their hair up every time they associate the need for change with the term quality.

Finally, the resistance to change is tied to how it is presented. As someone once said, "No one cares how much you know until they know how much you care." When change is suggested by a person perceived as non-caring or by one who has a self-serving agenda, many people will simply resist.

3.   Why do some people openly embrace change?

There exists another group of individuals in an organization that are usually in favor of changes and improvements.   Reasons for welcoming change are as diverse as those for resisting change.   Some individuals may see a proposed change as a potential for advancement, a chance for new learning, or an avenue for new growth.   In other cases, individuals are influenced through team spirit, peer pressure or by strong organization pressures.   Individuals who have been very discontent with the "status quo" may see the change as an opportunity for a better future because of their concern over such issues as the downsizing of the business or a lack of personal fulfillment.

There are also people who have a reputation for being the first to try new things.   These people might be characterized as having a "pioneering" spirit and can be counted on to readily accept new ideas.

4.   Is change always necessary?

No! If everything is in a constant state of change we border on chaos.   Change only for the sake of change must be avoided. Furthermore, individuals and organizations need times of stability to evaluate where they are.   That is difficult to do if we're always changing.

> *"We trained hard. But it seemed that every time we were beginning to form up we would be reorganized. ... I was to learn later in life that we tend to meet any new situation by reorganizing, and a wonderful method it can be for creating the illusion of progress while producing confusion, inefficiency and demoralization."*

Petronius Arbitar, 66 A.D.

On the flip side, perfection is something we should always be striving for and as such, change should always continue to take place over the long term. It is important, therefore, to discern when stability is needed versus when to push for positive change. This issue is developed further in questions 5 and 6.

5. What are the key ingredients for successful change?

In order to see successful change take place we will need some measure of the following three ingredients.

a)   a *need* for change

b)   a *vision* for what the change will do for the individual and the organization

c)   a *plan* to make change take place

6. How do we manage the three ingredients in question 5?

Regardless of our natural response to change or our resistance/willingness to change, unless we clearly see the need for change, it is illogical to pursue it. To develop the need for change, suppose we ask the following question, "What is the cost of doing nothing?" The answer to this question may be difficult to obtain. However, if we do not thoroughly address this question early on, the change process will be painful and may be impossible. Ideally, we should have a task force of key individuals in our organization to explore this question. Motorola did something similar in the late 70's and early 80's. By benchmarking off the Japanese, Motorola saw their competition at defect rates and cycle time levels far superior to theirs. The Japanese used these metrics to estimate waste (or Cost of Poor Quality) in their organizations while Motorola (at that time) did not. This benchmarking exercise provided the facts and data which enabled the senior executive to develop strong convictions for change, i.e., the cost of doing nothing was estimated to be very large in terms of dollars. It is, however, not enough for only senior management to understand the need to change. Employees must have access to information about their organization that will enable them also to see the need to change.

> *"If a worker lacks information, he will lack both incentive and means to improve a business."*

Peter Drucker

Thus, we must train employees to act like business people and not just hired hands.

After seeing a need for change, the next step is to visualize what we want to look like when the change is complete. This step requires the need to set measurable stretch goals. Small change is difficult to differentiate from no change at all, whereas stretch goals produce the possibility for substantial improvement. Again for organizations such as Motorola, Texas Instruments, General Electric, AlliedSignal and others, these goals are focused on metrics such as defect rates, cycle times, cost of poor quality and other measurable levels of customer satisfaction.

> *"People seldom hit what they do not aim at."*

Henry David Thoreau

Once we establish what we want to look like when the change is complete, the only missing ingredient is the plan to make the change take place. Here is where the guts of KBM fit in. Any plan for successful change that does not address increased knowledge of products, services, processes, people, suppliers and customers is destined to produce poor results. We suggest a careful study of the questions managers need to answer and managers need to ask. Because of their importance, these questions have been presented in this text three times. The most recent presentation of these questions is in Appendices A and B.

> *"Without questions, there is not learning."*

W. Edwards Deming

Successful change requires that we make every effort to evaluate, develop, and communicate the *need*, *vision* and *plan*. If we are not making every effort to change, we better go back to the *need* because we obviously do not understand the "cost of not changing, i.e., the cost of doing nothing." As a final note, be aware that frustration levels will get really high when we continue to push *vision* and *plan* on those who do not see the *need*.

7.   How can successful change be sustained?

The most difficult part of change is getting started; however, another challenge is sustaining a positive change. It is our belief that if the need, vision and plan are clearly communicated, most people will want to change. For those who still need a little encouragement, the best tools are the scorecard and the reward system. Most people love to win at what they attempt in life. Those who are ambivalent to winning will still want to be rewarded for what they do. Maintaining change can be as simple as keeping the right score, posting it, and tying it to the reward system.[*]

> *"If there is no reward,*
> *why does anybody give a damn?"*

Roger McDivitt
Patagonia Manager

References and Additional Readings:

Bridges, William. *Managing Transitions: Making the Most of Change.* Addison-Wesley Publishing Company, Reading, MA, 1991.

Carr, D.K., Hard, K.J., Trahant, W.J. *Managing the Change Process: a Field Book for Change Agents, Consultants, Team Leaders, and Reengineering Managers.* McGraw-Hill, New York, NY, 1996.

Case, John. *Open-Book Management. The Coming Business Revolution.* HarperCollins Publishers, Inc., New York, NY, 1997.

Conner, Daryl. *Managing at the Speed of Change: How Resilient Managers Succeed and Prosper Where Others Fail.* Villard Books, New York, NY, 1995.

Costello, Sheila J. *Managing Change in the Workplace.* Irwin Professional Publishing, Burr Ridge, IL, 1994.

---

[*]See Appendix D to learn how Jack Welch (GE's CEO) uses the reward system to make Six Sigma successful.

Fiman, Byron. *Accelerating Change: The Missing Ingredient to Effective Quality Improvement.* Implementation Management Associates, Inc., Brighton, CO, 1995.

Flecher, Tom, and Hunt, Jim. *Software Engineering and Case: Bridging the Culture Gap.* McGraw-Hill, New York, NY, 1993.

Hutton, David W. *The Change Agents' Handbook: A Survival Guide for Quality Improvement Champions.* ASQC Quality Press, Milwaukee, WI, 1994.

Joyner, Bryan. *Fourth Generation Management*, McGraw-Hill, New York, NY, 1994.

Kotter, John P. *Leading Change*, Harvard Business School Press, Boston, MA, 1996.

Kubler-Ross, Elisabeth. *On Death and Dying.* Macmillan Press, New York, NY, 1969.

Appendix D

SIX SIGMA FOR MANUFACTURING AND NON-MANUFACTURING PROCESSES

Six Sigma is a quality improvement and business strategy that began in the 1980's at Motorola. Emphasis is on reducing defects to less than 4 per million, reducing cycle time with aggressive goals such as 30-50% reduction per year, and reducing costs to dramatically impact the bottom line. The statistical and problem solving tools are similar to other modern day quality improvement strategies. However, Six Sigma stresses the *application* of these tools in a methodical and systematic fashion to gain knowledge that leads to breakthrough improvements with dramatic, measurable impact on the bottom line. The secret ingredient that really makes Six Sigma work is the infrastructure that is built within the organization. It is this infrastructure that motivates and produces a Six Sigma culture or "thought process" throughout the entire organization. The power of a Six Sigma approach is best described by proven return-on-investment (ROI) as shown next from Motorola, AlliedSignal, and General Electric (GE).

Motorola ROI

1987-1994

- Reduced in-process defect levels by a factor of 200.
- Reduced manufacturing costs by $1.4 billion.
- Increased employee production on a dollar basis by 126%.
- Increased stockholders share value fourfold.

AlliedSignal ROI

1992-1996

- $1.4 Billion cost reduction.
- 14% growth per quarter.
- 520% price/share growth.
- Reduced new product introduction time by 16%.
- 24% bill/cycle reduction.

General Electric ROI

1995-1998

- Company wide savings of over $1 Billion.
- Estimated annual savings to be $6.6 Billion by the year 2000.

Based on the number of articles written this past year about GE and its CEO, Jack Welch, GE has now become the standard bearer for how Six Sigma is implemented to successfully drive positive bottom line impact along with recognized "World Class" status. Other highly respected and successful companies such as SONY are benchmarking off of GE and implementing a similar strategy.

The companies mentioned thus far are certainly well known for their engineering and manufacturing excellence. What is not as well known is their view of the importance of Six Sigma in non-manufacturing or transactional areas. Bob Galvin, former President and CEO of Motorola, has stated that the lack of initial Six Sigma emphasis in the non-manufacturing areas was a mistake that cost Motorola at least $5 Billion over a 4-year period. It is common these days to hear comments like, "Yes, Company X has a great product, but they sure are a pain to do business with!" Consequently, Jack Welch is mandating Six Sigma in all aspects of his business, most recently in sales and other transactional (non-manufacturing) processes. Unfortunately, the typical response from non-manufacturing employees has been, "We're different. Six Sigma makes sense for manufacturing but does not apply to us!" This is simply an excuse in order to avoid being held to the same accountability standards as manufacturing.

The point to be made here is that any process can be represented as a set of inputs which, when used together, generates a corresponding set of outputs. An abbreviated pharmaceutical tablet manufacturing process might appear as shown next:

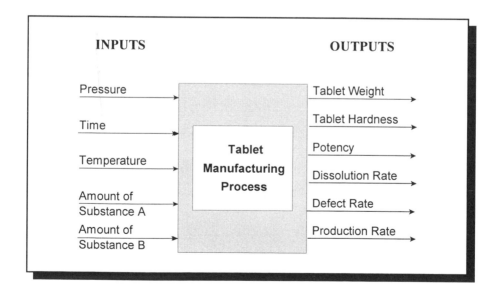

Transactional organizations simply are not accustomed to looking at their processes in this manner and thus will struggle a little in developing a similar abbreviated diagnosis of a transactional process. An Input-Process-Output (IPO) diagram for a sales process is shown below:

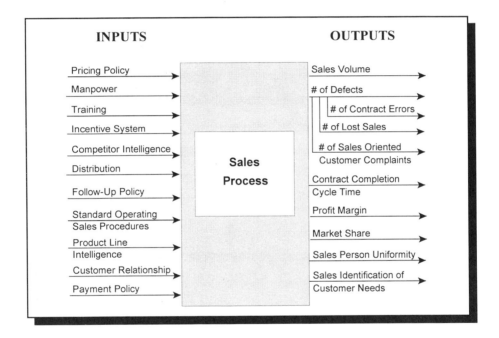

Thus, a process is a process, regardless of the type of organization or function. All processes have inputs and outputs. All processes have customers and suppliers, and all processes exhibit variation. Since the purpose of Six Sigma is to gain breakthrough knowledge on how to improve processes to do things **Better**, **Faster**, and at **Lower Cost**, it applies to everyone. Furthermore, since processes such as sales have historically relied less on scientific methods than engineering and manufacturing, the need for Six Sigma (i.e., a structured and systematic methodology) is even stronger here. This has been and is being recognized by World Class CEO's such as Bob Galvin, Larry Bossidy, and Jack Welch.

The method to implement Six Sigma for non-manufacturing processes is simple: the same way we implement it for engineering and manufacturing processes at Motorola, Texas Instruments, GE, Lockheed Martin, Corning, Sony, etc., with only slight modifications. These modifications are typically confined to the type and depth of statistical tools that need to be included in the training. Obviously, the slant on applications must also be directed toward the non-manufacturing processes.

A specific strategy for Six Sigma manufacturing and non-manufacturing processes would look similar to what is shown below:

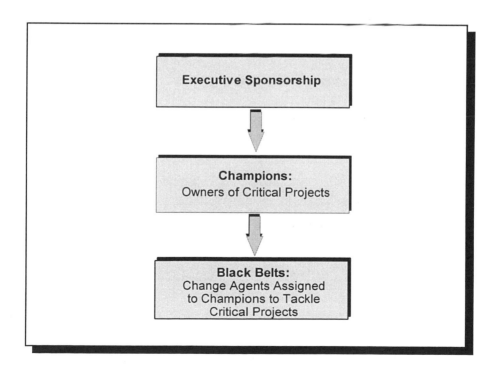

The executives must have a total commitment to the implementation of Six Sigma and accomplish the following:

1. Establish a Six Sigma Leadership Team.

2. Identify key business issues.

3. Assign Champions to each key business issue.

4. Assist the Champions and Leadership Team in identifying critical projects that are tied to the key business issues.

5. Assist the Champions and Leadership Team in selecting Black Belt candidates.

6. Allocate time for change agents (Black Belts) to make breakthrough improvements.

7. Set aggressive Six Sigma goals.

8. Incorporate Six Sigma performance into the reward system.

9. Direct finance to validate all Six Sigma ROI.

10. Evaluate the corporate culture to determine if intellectual capital is being infused into the company.

11. Continuously evaluate the Six Sigma implementation and deployment process and make changes if necessary.

The roles of the Leadership Team, Champions, and Black Belts are defined next.

COMPARISON OF ROLES

	BLACK BELT	CHAMPION	LEADERSHIP TEAM
PROFILE	• technically oriented • respected by peers and management • master of basic and advanced tools	• senior manager • respected leader and mentor of business issues • strong proponent of Six Sigma who asks the right questions	• highly visible in company • trained in Six Sigma • respected leaders and mentors for Black Belts
ROLE	• leads strategic, high impact process improvement projects • change agent • trains and coaches on tools and analysis • teaches and mentors cross-functional team members • full-time project leader • converts gains into $	• selects projects and Black Belts • provides resources and strong leadership for projects • inspires a shared vision • establishes plan and creates infrastructure • develops metrics • converts gains into $	• develop a training Master Plan to implement Six Sigma • schedule training • select projects and Black Belts • determine certification requirements and certify Black Belts • develop a Black Belt network to enhance communication • review and improve the Six Sigma process
TRAINING	• three to four 1-week sessions with three to six weeks between sessions to apply to project • project review in every session	• 4 days of Champion training • Six Sigma development and implementation plan	• one day of Basics of Six Sigma training or four days of Champion training
NUMBERS	• 1 per 50 employees (2 %)	• 1 per business group or major working site	• 4 - 6 member team

The overall approach to obtaining the **right kind of knowledge** is focused on finding the **answers to the 14 questions** shown next. These questions, which are partitioned into a strategy (**P**rioritize, **C**haracterize, **O**ptimize, and **R**ealize) to be implemented in 4 phases (**M**easure, **A**nalyze, **I**mprove, **C**ontrol), form the Six Sigma Project Master Strategy.

SIX SIGMA PROJECT MASTER STRATEGY

Prioritize — Characterize

1. What processes are you responsible for? Who is the owner of these processes? Who are the team members? How well does the team work together?

2. Which processes have the highest priority for improvement? How did you come to this conclusion? Where is the data that supports this conclusion?

3. How is the process performed?

4. What are the process performance measures? Why? How accurate and precise is the measurement system?

5. What are the customer driven specifications for all of the performance measures? How good or bad is the current performance? Show me the data. What are the improvement goals for the process?

6. What are all the sources of variability in the process? Show me what they are.

7. Which sources of variability do you control? How do you control them and how is it documented?

8. Are any sources of variability supplier-dependent? If so, what are they, who's the supplier and what's being done about it?

9. What are the key variables that affect the average and variation of the measures of performance? How do you know this? Show me the data.

10. What are the relationships between the measures of performance and the key variables? Do any key variables interact? How do you know for sure? Show me the data.

Measure — Analyze

SIX SIGMA PROJECT MASTER STRATEGY (Cont.)

Optimize	Realize
11. What setting for the key variables will optimize the measures of performance? How do you know this? Show me the data. 12. For the optimal setting of the key variables, what kind of variability exists in the performance measures? How do you know? Show me the data.	13. How much improvement has the process shown in the last 6 months? How do you know this? Show me the data. 14. How much time and/or money have your efforts saved or generated for the company? How did you document all of your efforts? Show me the data.
Improve	**Control**

The Six Sigma tools and methodology must be taught to Champions, Black Belts and other managers at a level they can grasp and feel confident to apply. A proven instructional approach developed by Air Academy Associates is shown next:

A **K**eep-**I**t-**S**imple-**S**tatistically (**KISS**) approach is used, with the intention to avoid statistical complexity. Statistics is not presented as an "end", but rather the means to gaining knowledge for making good decisions which are critical for success. There are a variety of Six Sigma tools and techniques, and we will use the "Present/Practice/Apply/Review" instructional strategy. That is, we will *present* a tool or method, give you a chance to *practice* that tool in class, then have you *apply* that tool to your project, and finally have you *review* the results of the application to your project. A final report will be written to document your success story and its impact to the company's bottom line.

Another critical piece to a successful Six Sigma experience is the reward structure. Recall that many companies struggled to engage the entire organization in implementing TQM. To overcome this problem, Jack Welch has made the following statements:

1. To get promoted you must be Six Sigma trained.

2. Forty percent of top management bonuses are tied to Six Sigma goals.

3. Stock options are tied to Six Sigma performance.

As you can imagine, General Electric has very few problems engaging the entire organization in its Six Sigma initiative.

Thus, the modern day Six Sigma movement has fully embraced a Knowledge Based Management approach. Numerous companies, such as General Electric and Sony, are demonstrating that this approach has a high return on investment. This new and improved Six Sigma business strategy is much more powerful than the original Six Sigma developed at Motorola. For more information on the power of Six Sigma, see General Electric's 1997 Annual Report in which ⅔ of the report is devoted to this subject.

Glossary of Terms

affinity diagram   a technique for organizing individual pieces of information into groups or broader categories.

average of a sample ($\bar{x}$)   also called the sample mean, it is the arithmetic average of all of the sample values. It is calculated by adding all of the sample values together and dividing by the number of elements (n) in the sample.

bar chart   a graphical method which depicts how data fall into different categories.

benchmarking   an activity which encompasses the search for and implementation of best practices.

black belt   a key person who is trained to execute critical projects and deliver breakthrough enhancements to the bottom line; also a change agent, doer, and catalyst.

brainstorming   a technique used by a group to generate a large number of ideas in a short time period.

capability of a process   a measure of quality usually expressed as C_p, C_{pk}, or defects per million (dpm). It is obtained by comparing the actual process with the specification limit(s).

cause and effect diagram   a pictorial diagram in the shape of a fishbone showing all possible variables that could affect a given process output measure.

central tendency   a measure of the point about which a group of values is clustered; two measures of central tendency are the mean, and the median.

champion   a Director or VP-level manager who acts as the sponsor/ owner of a project and as a mentor/helper for Black Belts.

characteristic   a process output which can be measured and monitored for control and capability.

class interval   each cell or subinterval of a histogram.

classes   cells or intervals in a frequency distribution or histogram.

common causes of variation   those sources of variability in a process which are truly random, i.e., inherent in the process itself.

common sense   the demonstration and application of traits shown to be associated with critical thinking and good judgement.

control chart   the most powerful tool of statistical process control. It consists of a run chart, together with statistically determined upper and lower control limits and a centerline.

control limits   upper and lower bounds in a control chart that are determined by the process itself. They can be used to detect special causes of variation. They are usually set at ± 3 standard deviations from the centerline which is usually the mean.

control of a process   a process is said to be in a state of statistical control if the process exhibits only random variation (as opposed to special causes of variation and/or variation from known sources). When monitoring a process with control charts, a state of control is exhibited when all points remain between the control limits without any abnormal (non-random) patterns.

correlation coefficient   a measure of the linear relationship between two variables.

cost of poor quality (COPQ)   the costs associated with any activity that is not doing the right thing right the first time. COPQ includes, but is not limited to, such things as rework, scrap, waste, useless meetings, etc.

C_p a process capability measure defined as the ratio of specification width (USL - LSL) to process width (6σ).

C_{pk} during process capability studies, C_{pk} is an index used to compare the natural tolerances of a process with the specification limits. If C_{pk} is negative, the process mean is outside the specification limits; if C_{pk} is between 0 and 1, then the natural tolerances of the process fall outside the spec limits. If C_{pk} is larger than 1, the natural tolerances fall completely within the spec limits. A value of 1.33 or greater is usually desired.

customer   anyone who uses or consumes a product or service, whether internal or external to the providing organization or provider.

customer needs and expectations   customer wants, desires, wishes, and demands for products and services translated into measurable indicators of cost, quality (various dimensions), and delivery (time and quantity). Often referred to as customer requirements.

D1-9000 an aerospace industry (Boeing specific) standard for documenting quality improvement systems, to include the proper use of statistical tools.

design of experiments (DOE)   generally, it is the discipline of using an efficient, structured, and proven approach to interrogating a process (or product) for the purpose of maximizing the gain in process or product knowledge.

dispersion of a sample   the tendency of the values in a sample to differ from each other. Dispersion is commonly expressed in terms of the range of the sample (difference between the lowest and highest values) or by the standard deviation.

experimental design   specifically, it is purposeful changes to the inputs (factors) of a process in order to observe corresponding changes in the outputs (responses).

factor   an input to a process which can be manipulated during experimentation.

failure mode and effects analysis (FMEA)   a procedure used to identify and assess risks associated with potential product or process failure modes.

fault tree analysis (FTA)   a technique for evaluating the possible causes which might lead to the failure of a product. For each possible failure, the possible causes of the failure are determined; then the situations leading to those causes are determined; and so forth, until all paths leading to possible failures have been traced. The result is a flow chart for the failure process. Plans to deal with each path can then be made.

fishbone diagram   see cause and effect diagram.

flowchart   a graphic representation that symbolically shows the sequential activities and branching in a process that produces an output.

FOCUS   an acronym for a 5-step breakdown of the PDCA cycle's planning phase. **F**ind a process to improve. **O**rganize a team. **C**larify current knowledge. **U**nderstand causes of variation. **S**elect the process improvement that we plan to do.

gage capability study   collecting data to assess how much variation is in the measurement system itself and to compare it to the total process variation.

green belt   a person trained to provide technical assistance to a Black Belt and/or undertake projects of lesser scope than a Black Belt project.

histogram   a bar chart that depicts the frequencies (or heights of the bars) of numerical or measurement categories.

input a resource consumed, utilized, or added in a process that produces a product or delivers a service.

input-process-output (IPO) diagram a visual representation of a process where inputs are represented by input arrows to a box (which represents the process) and outputs are shown using arrows emanating out of the box.

Ishikawa diagram see cause and effect diagram.

ISO-9000 an international standard for documenting quality assurance systems.

KISS Keep It Simple Statistically.

least squares a method of curve-fitting that defines the "best" fit as the one that minimizes the sum of the squared deviations of the data points from the fitted curve.

lower control limit (LCL) for control charts: the limit above which the process subgroup statistics ($\bar{x}$, R, sigma) must remain when the process is in control. Typically, 3 standard deviations below the centerline.

lower specification limit (LSL) the lowest value of a product dimension or measurement which is acceptable.

matrix a graphic that is used to show the relationship between two or more groups of characteristics, ideas, or issues.

mean the average of a set of values. We usually use $\bar{x}$ or $\bar{y}$ to denote a sample mean, whereby we use the Greek letter μ to denote a population mean.

measures of central tendency numerical measures that depict the center of a data set. The most commonly used measures are the mean and the median.

median the middle value of a data set when the values are arranged in either ascending or descending order.

metric a performance measure that is considered to be a key pulse point of an organization. It should be linked to goals or objectives and carefully monitored.

mission a statement defining the organization's unique purpose.

modeling design a type of designed experiment whose primary purpose is to build a mathematical model that characterizes the relationship between key input factors and a critical response variable.

multiple regression a model where several independent variables are used to predict one dependent variable.

natural tolerances of a process 3 standard deviations on either side of the center point (mean value). In a normally distributed process, the natural tolerances encompass 99.73% of all measurements.

nominal group technique a structured method that a group can use to generate and rank order a list of ideas or items.

non-value activities any activity performed in producing a product or delivering a service that does not add value, where value is defined as something for which a customer would be willing to pay.

normal distribution the distribution characterized by the smooth, bell-shaped curve.

out of control   a process is said to be out of control if it exhibits variations larger than its control limits or shows a systematic pattern of variation.

output   a product produced or a service delivered by a process. It is often measured in terms of the quantity and quality of product or service delivered that meets a certain requirement, such as cost, quality (dimensions), and delivery (time and quantity) requirements.

paradigm   a set of boundaries (perhaps consciously, subconsciously, or even unconsciously defined) that form the limits of behavior, opinions, and decision-making.

Pareto chart   a bar chart for attribute (or categorical) data that is presented in descending order of frequency or monetary loss.

PDCA   the **P**lan-**D**o-**C**heck-**A**ct cycle (also known as the Shewhart or Deming cycle) is a repeatable four-phase implementation strategy for process improvement.

process   an activity which blends a set of inputs for the purpose of producing a product, providing a service, or performing a task.

process capability   comparing actual process performance with process specification limits. There are various measures of process capability, such as C_p, C_{pk}, and dpm (defects per million).

process characterization   demonstrating the ability to thoroughly understand a process, to include the specific relationship between the outputs and the inputs of a process.

process control   a process is said to be in control or it is a stable, predictable process if all special causes of variation have been removed. Only common causes or natural variation remain in the process.

process flow diagram   see flowchart.

process validation   establishing documented evidence which provides a high degree of assurance that a specific process will consistently produce a product that meets its pre-determined specifications and quality characteristics.

QS-9000   a U.S. automotive industry standard for documenting quality improvement systems, to include the proper use of statistical tools.

quality characteristic   a particular aspect of a product which relates to its ability to perform its intended function.

quality function deployment (QFD) a systematic process used to integrate customer requirements into every aspect of the design and delivery of products and services.

Quality Systems Review (QSR)   Motorola's standard for documenting quality improvement systems, to include the proper use of statistical tools.

range   a measure of the variability in a data set. It is a single value, namely the difference between the largest and smallest values in a data set.

regression analysis   a statistical technique for determining the mathematical relation between a measured quantity and the variables it depends on.

regression line   the line that is fit to a set of data points by using the method of least squares.

repeatability (of a measurement)   the extent to which repeated measurements of a particular object with a particular instrument produce the same value.

rework   activity required to correct for defects produced by a process.

rule of thumb (ROT) a simplified, practical procedure that can be used in place of a formal statistical test that will produce approximately the same result.

run chart a basic graphical tool that charts a process over time, recording either individual readings, averages, ranges, standard deviations, etc., over time.

scatter diagram a chart in which one variable is plotted against another to determine if there is a correlation between the two variables. Scatter diagrams can be used to verify cause-and-effect relationships, but a strong correlation does not necessarily indicate such a relationship because a third factor may be the causal factor.

scatterplot a two-dimensional plot for displaying bivariate data. See scatter diagram.

screening design a type of designed experiment whose primary purpose is to separate the significant factors from the insignificant factors.

sigma (σ) the standard deviation of a statistical population.

sigma capability a commonly used measure of process capability that represents the number of standard deviations between the center of a process and the closest specification limit. Sometimes referred to as sigma level.

six sigma is a quality improvement and business strategy that began in the 1980's at Motorola. Emphasis is on reducing defects, reducing cycle time with aggressive goals, and reducing costs to dramatically impact the bottom line. It involves establishing an organizational infrastructure together with a repeatable methodology and tools to accomplish business objectives.

SOP standard operating procedure. A set of prescribed or established actions or methods that are followed in order to control variability in a process.

special causes of variation those non-random causes of variation that can be detected by the use of control charts and good process documentation.

specification limits the bounds of acceptable values for a given product or process. They should be customer driven.

stability of a process a process is said to be stable if it shows no recognizable pattern of change and no special causes of variation are present.

standard deviation one of the most common measures of variability in a data set or in a population. It is the square root of the variance.

statistical control of a process a process is said to be in a state of statistical control when it exhibits only random variation.

statistical process control (SPC) the use of basic graphical and statistical methods for measuring, analyzing, and controlling the variation of a process for the purpose of continuously improving the process.

stretch goal a goal not easily attainable, yet not impossible, designed to create out-of-the box thinking to achieve breakthrough improvement.

survey a means of gathering data on people, processes, products, and organizations. It is usually accomplished via questionnaires, interviews, etc.

teamwork cooperative effort on the part of members of a group or team to achieve a common goal.

total quality management (TQM)   a management philosophy of integrated controls, including engineering, purchasing, financial administration, marketing and manufacturing, to ensure customer satisfaction and economical cost of quality.

trend   a gradual, systematic change over time or some other variable.

two-level design   an experiment where all factors are set at one of two levels, denoted as low and high (-1 and +1).

upper control limit (UCL)   for control charts: the upper limit below which a process statistic ($\bar{x}$, R, etc.) must remain to be in control. Typically this value is 3 standard deviations above the centerline.

upper specification limit (USL)   the highest value of a product dimension or measurement which is acceptable.

variability   a generic term that refers to the property of a metric (or key measurement) to take on different values.

variables   quantities which are subject to change or variability.

variance   a specifically defined mathematical measure of variability in a data set or population. It is the square of the standard deviation.

variation   see variability.

vision   ideals, hopes, and dreams that bring meaning to what we do. It provides the reason for an organization's being.

$\bar{x}$ and R charts   for variables data: control charts which plot the average and range of subgroups of data.

References

Blaha, Robert B. *Beyond Survival. Creating Prosperity Through People*. Air Academy Press, Colorado Springs, CO, 1995.

Brelin, H.K., Davenport, K.S., Jennings, L.P., and Murphy, P.F. *Focused Quality: Managing for Results*. St. Lucie Press, Delray Beach, FL, 1994.

Business Week. *How Jack Welch Runs GE* (article by John A. Byrne). June 8, 1998.

Deming, W. Edwards. *Out of the Crisis*. MIT Center for Advanced Engineering Study, Cambridge, MA, 1986.

Ennis, R. "Critical Thinking and Subject Specificity." *Educational Researcher*, Vol. 18, No. 3, 1989.

Hutton, David W. *The Change Agents' Handbook: A Survival Guide for Quality Improvement Champions*. ASQC Quality Press, Milwaukee, WI, 1994.

Ishikawa, Kaoru. *Guide to Quality Control*. Asian Productivity Organization, Tokyo, Japan, 1982.

Ishikawa, Kaoru. *What is Total Quality Control?* Prentice Hall, Englewood Cliffs, NJ, 1985.

Joyner, Bryan. *Fourth Generation Management*, McGraw-Hill, New York, NY, 1994.

Juran, J.M. *Juran on Leadership for Quality*. The Free Press, New York, NY, 1989.

Juran, J.M. *Juran on Planning for Quality*. The Free Press, New York, NY, 1988.

Kiemele, Mark J., Schmidt, Stephen R., and Berdine, Ronald J. *Basic Statistics: Tools for Continuous Improvement* (4th ed). Air Academy Press, Colorado Springs, CO, 1997.

Lam, K.D., Watson, Frank D., and Schmidt, Stephen R. *Total Quality: A Textbook of Strategic Quality, Leadership & Planning*. Air Academy Press, Colorado Springs, CO, 1991.

Schmidt, Stephen R., Cheek, T., and Kiemele, M. "Does TQM Have Return On Investment—If Not, Why Not?" *Quality Observer*, May 1994.

Schmidt, Stephen R. and Launsby, Robert G. *Understanding Industrial Designed Experiments*, (4th ed). Air Academy Press, Colorado Springs, CO, 1993.

Stamatis, D.H. *Failure Mode and Effect Analysis*. ASQC Quality Press, Milwaukee, WI, 1995.

Walton, Mary. *The Deming Management Method*. The Putnam Publishing Group, 1986.

Welch, Jack. *1997 GE Annual Report.*

Index

A

Affinity Diagram 124-125
Arbitar, Petronious 187
Average of a Sample ($\bar{x}$) . . . 139

B

Bacon, Francis 19
Baldrige
   criteria 188, 191
   performance 13-14
Bar Chart 135, 144
Barrett, Craig 6
Barriers to Quality
   Improvement 55-57,
   124-125
Benchmarking 126
Billing Process 76
Bivariate Data 154
Black Belt 18, 50, 51, D-7
Brainstorming 84-85,
   124, 178
Buetow, Richard C. 15

C

Cause and Effect
   diagram 127-129,
   140, 178
   relationship 155
Central Tendency . . . 135, 140
Champion 50, D-7

Change Management 161,
   190, Appendix C
Chowdhary, Rai 16
Chemical Analysis Process . 177
Class Interval 136
CNX 130, 138, 140
Common Sense 3, 8,
   34, 57, 67, 130-131
Composite Material
   Process 77
Control Chart 85, 166, 174
Control Limits . . 167, 169, 174
   zones 166
Correlation 155-156
Cost of Poor Quality
   (COPQ) 33, 42,
   72, 82
C_p 146
C_{pk} 39, 107,
   120, 146, 148, 164
Creativity 110, 112
Critical Thinking 130-131
Customer 38-39
   driven specifications 47,
   70, 88, 105
   needs 56, 69, 73,
   98, 102, 106
   requirements 18, 73, 152
   satisfaction 81
Cycle Time 17, 37,
   39, 59, 62, 81, 120

D

D1-9000 . . . . 54, 112, 188, 191

Deming, W. Edwards 21, 24, 28, 65, 80

fourteen points 24-27

philosophy 24

Design of Experiments (DOE) 116, 163, 177-186

Diderot, Denis 185

dpm 146-147, 164

Drucker, Peter 9

d'Arbeloff, Alexander 18

E

Empowerment 110, 112

Executive's View 164

Experimental Design . . 177-186

F

Factor 178-179, 181-184

Factors and Levels 179

Failure Mode and Effect Analysis (FMEA) . . . 132-133

Fault Tree Analysis (FTA) 134

Feedback 32, 44

Fishbone Diagram 127

Fisher, George 15

Flowchart 149

FOCUS 82-84

Franklin, Benjamin 163

G

Gage Capability 105, 175

Galvin, Chris 15

Garvin, David 3

Gaudin, Jan 42

Gillman, Sid 23

Green Belt 18

H

Histogram 85, 135-137

House of Success 192

I

Ingenuity 110, 112

Input Factors . . . 117, 178-183

Input-Process-Output (IPO) Diagram 74-78, 137-138

Ishikawa

diagram 127

Kaoru 21-23, 29, 109

list of things top management must do 30-31

philosophy 29

ISO-9000 . . . . 54, 112, 188, 191

J

Jennings, Lyell 190
Johnson, Samuel 12, 195
Juran, Joseph M. 15,
21-23, 29, 31, 63, 65
philosophy 28
10 steps to quality
improvement 28-29

K

Kant, Immanuel 145
KBM
approach 190-191
key ingredients 4
paradigm 189
philosophy 31, 191, 192
process 90
scorecard 194
strategy 88
Keep It Simple Statistically
(KISS) 5, 6, 8,
16-17
Kirkpatrick's Model 52-53
Knowledge 3, 5
Knowledge Based Management
see KBM

L

Langer, Susanne K. 187
Lasch, Christopher 194
Lasorda, Tommy 96
LCL (Lower Control
Limit) 167-173
Lombardi, Vince 58, 193

Lord Kelvin 78
LSL (Lower Specification
Limit) 146-148,
174, 177, 184
Lukens Steel 53

M

Machining Process 76
Mail Sorting Process 77
Malcolm Baldrige Quality
Award 54, 65, 188
Manufacturing Injection
Molded Parts 138
Matrix 59, 101-103,
179-180, 183
Matrix Development
Approach 101-103
Matsushita, Konosuke . . . 92-93
McDonald, Bill 86
Mean 139, 141,
148, 178
Measurement System Standard
Deviation 176
Measures of Central
Tendency 139-140
Measures of Dispersion 141
Median 139-140
Mentor 50, 57
Metric(s) 16, 39, 52,
101, 144, 163
Mission 74,
86, 142
Mission Statement 34-37

Modeling Design 183
Mooney, Kenneth O. 92

N

National Institute of Standards
   and Technology 38
Natural Variability 174
Noise Factors 175
Nominal Group Technique
   (NGT) 142-143

O

Orthogonality 179, 181
Out of Control 98, 109,
   166, 171
Outliers 140, 175, 176
Output 74, 75,
   81, 137, 178, 179, 181

P

Paradigm 187-188
Pareto
   chart 144-145
   principle 144
PCOR 90
PDCA 80, 84-85
Practitioner's View 165
Process 25-27, 46,
   59, 78, 82, 84-86, 88, 91, 95,
     102, 107-108, 119, 138, 151,
     166-168, 172, 178

Process
   capability 146, 148,
     164, 174, 184
   capability measurements
     146-148
   characterization 54,
     188, 191
   control 163
   flow diagram 83,
     102, 140, 149-151
   knowledge 46, 79,
     163, 165-166, 177, 185-186
   validation 54, 111, 188
   variation 83

Q

QS-9000 . . . . 111, 188
Quality Characteristics 137
Quality Function Deployment
   (QFD) 70, 152
Quality Improvement
   Puzzle 1, 191
Quality Manager's View . . . 164
Quality Systems Review
   (QSR) 188
Questions Managers Need to
   Answer 3, 31,
     32-66, 193, App. B
Questions Managers Need to
   Ask 3, 41,
     88-122, App. A

R

Range 141, 168-169
Regression 155-156
   analysis 116-117, 156
   line 156
Return On Investment
   (ROI) 18-20,
   33, 53, 186-188
Rework 177
Riemann, Curtis 38
Rule of Thumb (ROT) 176
Run Chart 85, 153

S

Sample
   mean 139
   median 139
   standard deviation 141
   variance 141
Scatter Diagram 85,
   154-156
Schaller, D.A. 69-70
Schmidt, Fred 66
Scholtes, Peter 79
Scorecard 50,
   52-53, 60-61, 193-194
   on COPQ 120-121
Screening Design 180, 182
Shakespeare 123
Shewhart, Walter A. 80
Sigma (σ) 105, 147
Silich, Bert 17

Six Sigma 1, 8, 18-19, 66,
   86, 88, 122, 148, 215, App. D
Software
   development errors . . . 69-70
   lifecycle 78
   quality 69
Sources of Variability . . 47, 89,
   107-110
Special Causes 169-171
Standard Deviation . . . 117-119,
   141
Standard Operating Procedures
   (SOPs) 81, 109-110,
   128, 140, 175
Stata, Ray 18
Statistical Process Control
   (SPC) 163, 166,
   176-186
Stretch Goals 62, 193
Supplier Quality Improvement
   Requirements 188
Survey 44, 55

T

Teamwork 26, 92,
   157-161
Tooker, Gary 15
Total Quality Management
   (TQM) 2, 110
Trend 40, 153
Tribus, Myron 45, 174

U

UCL (Upper Control
  Limit) 167-173
Ugly Facts of the 90's . . 10-12
USL (Upper Specification
  Limit) 146-148,
  174, 177-178

V

Van Sant, Bill 17, 53
Variability 109-110,
  181-183, 185
Variables 48, 89,
  107, 114-118, 127-128, 135,
  140, 154-156
Variance 127, 141, 176

Variation 128, 153, 175
  special causes of 171
Vision Statement 35
Vos Savant, Marilyn 189

W

Wells, H.G. 156
White, Joseph B. 40, 68

X

x̄ and R Charts 168-173

Y

Yates, W.D. 69, 70